W9-BDU-271

Fluid

Web

Typography

New
HUMBER LIBRARIES LAKESHORE CAMPUS
3199 Lakeshore Blvd West
TORONTO, ON.   M8V 1K8
DISCARD

Fluid Web Typography

Jason Cranford Teague

New Riders
1249 Eighth Street
Berkeley, CA 94710
510/524-2178

Find us on the Web at www.newriders.com
To report errors, please send a note to errata@peachpit.com

New Riders is an imprint of Peachpit, a division of Pearson Education

Copyright © 2010 Jason Cranford Teague

Project Editor:
Nancy Peterson

Development Editor:
Brenda McLaughlin

Technical Editor:
Christopher Schmitt

Production Coordinator:
Cory Borman

Production Assistant:
Danielle Foster

Copy Editor:
Elissa Rabellino

Compositor and Interior Design:
Jason Cranford Teague

Indexer:
Karin Arrigoni

Cover Design:
Mimi Heft with Jason Cranford Teague

Notice of Rights

All rights reserved. No part of this book may be reproduced or transmitted in any form by any means, electronic, mechanical, photocopying, recording, or otherwise, without the prior written permission of the publisher. For information on getting permission for reprints and excerpts, contact permissions@peachpit.com.

Notice of Liability

The information in this book is distributed on an "As Is" basis without warranty. While every precaution has been taken in the preparation of the book, neither the author nor Peachpit shall have any liability to any person or entity with respect to any loss or damage caused or alleged to be caused directly or indirectly by the instructions contained in this book or by the computer software and hardware products described in it.

Trademarks

Many of the designations used by manufacturers and sellers to distinguish their products are claimed as trademarks. Where those designations appear in this book, and Peachpit was aware of a trademark claim, the designations appear as requested by the owner of the trademark. All other product names and services identified throughout this book are used in editorial fashion only and for the benefit of such companies with no intention of infringement of the trademark. No such use, or the use of any trade name, is intended to convey endorsement or other affiliation with this book.

Printed and bound in the United States of America

ISBN 13: 978-0-321-67998-7
ISBN 10: 0-321-67998-9

9 8 7 6 5 4 3 2 1

Printed and bound in the United States of America

For Tara, Jocelyn & Dashiel

Thanks...

Dad & Nancy

Johnny

Pat & Red

Boyd, Dr. G. & Judy

Thomas, Archer & David

Heather C.

Douglas Adams

Carl Sagan

Trent Reznor

Matt Johnson

Neil Gaiman & Dave McKean

Joel Hodgson & the MST3K crew

Charles Dodgson & John Tenniel

The noise that kept me going...

NPR, Ted Talks, BBC 6 Music, Skepticality, Slice of SciFi, the Craig Charles Funk & Soul Show, the Ruts, B.B. King, Bat for Lashes, Amanda Palmer (AFP), Wilson Pickett, Carbon/Silicon, Rasputina, Kate Bush, Bryan Ferry, the Fixx, Jonathan Coulton, Oingo Boingo, Johnny Cash, Cocteau Twins, Ladytron, Marvin Gaye, Client, Cracker, Corduroy, Al Green, the Wombats, Electric Six, World Party, Skinny Puppy, the Cramps, Poprocket, Franz Ferdinand, the Long Blondes, Gogol Bordello, Mojo Nixon, Beck, and the Specials.

CONTENTS

FOREWORD

HAHAHAHAHA! That's me laughing at the current state of typography on the Web. LOL! What a joke.

I assure you it's a good-natured laugh, like an assuring guffaw, that says, "Oh can ya believe how silly we were? Working with just those ten core Web fonts for the first 15 years of the World Wide Web?" I can laugh because it's clear that everything's about to change, and we're on the cusp of a whole new treatment of type on the Internet. Hooray!

No longer will Web designers be stuck with a meager dozen fonts to work with. They've been held back for too long, and now they're about to feast on a broad new spectrum of typefaces to specify in Web pages. It reminds me of a ninja in training who is allowed to hold a bow, but who must train with that bow for seven years before he's given an arrow. He must have a complete understanding and familiarity with the bow before he's allowed to shoot a single arrow.

The Web designer has been given a limited number of fonts to work with all these years, so we all have a good understanding of the broader mechanics of what the Web is and how it works. The engineers, programmers, and network people have been in control for all this time. Now it's

Chank Diesel is an online typography pioneer who has been creating and distributing fonts on his Web site *chank.com* since 1996.

pretty clear how the Web works and how it's built, so we're ready to start adding embellishments. Like giving the designers new fonts to use.

New technologies are changing the way type is delivered to Web sites. Services like Typekit and Kernest that use the new `@font-face` CSS call now allow designers to embed any of thousands of fonts into Web pages. It's not gonna be pictures of type, like GIFs or JPEGs. Nor is it gonna be embedded in a Flash file in a page. The fonts will be embedded right in the text of your browser, allowing them to flow as real, searchable HTML in the content of your page. Search engines will be able to read the new fonts, just like they've been reading Courier and Times for all these years.

Web standards were fairly restrictive during the early days of the Web, and I think that's a good thing. It's allowed designers to focus on the big design issues, and not dawdle or dwell on the intricacies of what font will be used. But now that everybody's got a pretty good grasp on what a Web page basically looks like, we're ready to kick it up a notch with some fresh new type. It's gonna make a big impact on the Web we view every day.

For the best-designed Web pages, the changes will be hardly noticeable. Ideally, you shouldn't notice the font you're reading; you should read the words and message and not be distracted by the type style. But with a good sense of style and a modicum of restraint, Web typographers will be able to introduce pages with new type so that the reader doesn't notice it's a different font, but appreciates that the overall page feels better—more flavorful, fresher, and more exciting, through the use of tasteful typography.

Of course there will be atrocities coming soon. Designers will abuse these new functionalities, and make sites with a dozen fonts on one page. Or they might use overly ornate display fonts at substandard sizes to mark up paragraphs of body text. Typographic gaffes will be readily visible, but that should make it even clearer when you're looking at a smart Web page or a dumb one. For the discriminating reader, the typography will tell you immediately.

I'm ecstatic that *Fluid Web Typography* has come about, instructing you on all the technical basics of how to implement fonts in the new browsers. As a font designer, I can make all the great fonts I want, but it doesn't help me at all until people actually start to use them. It's been great seeing my fonts in books, magazines, advertising, and products over the years. But media are changing, and it seems pretty clear that people will be getting most of their information from the Web in the near future. So I need a way for Web designers to get my fonts working in the browsers that people will be looking at. This book tells you how to do it. Amen.

Good luck with the new world of fluid brave Web typography!

—CHANK DIESEL
www.chank.com
2009

PREFACE

◄ x

We are standing on the threshold of a revolution in Web typography. I'm not talking about a revolution in the Madison Avenue "revolutionary new sneaker" kind of way. I'm talking about a *real* revolution, where those without power wrangle it from those with power. That's what's happening today in Web typography: Small groups are solving problems that have plagued Web design since its creation, problems that the big players—the people who make the standards and the people who make the browsers—have been unable or unwilling to solve.

New techniques coupled with new Web browser capabilities promise to elevate Web typography from its current monotonous state into a compelling design discipline. For more than a decade, Web designers have endured a stagnation in typographic possibilities, primarily due to the almost nonexistent choices of typefaces available to them. While there is no technical reason why a font file cannot be downloaded just like an image file, the browser manufacturers have (until only recently) refused to support the most common font file formats.

That has all now changed.

In the 15 years that I have been a Web designer, I have rarely seen a time when something so
fundamental to Web design was about to change.
Browsers such as Firefox, Opera, and Safari now
include the ability to download both OpenType
and TrueType fonts. The only holdout is Microsoft
Internet Explorer, which currently holds the majority of the browser market. On the upside, IE
does support its own font file format for download (Embedded OpenType, or EOT). Many services are in development that will let you bridge
this gap between browsers, allowing you to select
from increasingly large lists of fonts.

The Web is about to undergo a massive transformation, typographically speaking. The question
is, are you ready for that transformation?

To manage the transition, you need to understand the fluid nature of Web typography. Because
the limits of setting type in browser windows are
onerous, many designers simply rely on the browsers' default styles rather than consider how to improve their typographic layout. Designers want certainty in a medium where certainty does not exist.

My original intention for this book was to
present all of the Web safe fonts; talk about the future of downloading fonts, which, at the time, only
Safari was supporting; and then talk about how to
use existing cross-browser CSS code to add scale,
contrast, emphasis, and rhythm to your text to
create your own typographic voice.

But a funny thing happened between the day I
started this book and the day I finished writing it:
The Web typography revolution began. To be fair,
it really started when Apple allowed Safari to include the ability to download and render Open-
Type and TrueType fonts in 2008, but that was only

the opening salvo. Since I started this book in the middle of 2009, the following has happened:

◉ Both Firefox and Opera have released browsers that support OpenType and TrueType fonts.

◉ Three Web font service bureaus have launched with cross-browser solutions. There are more on the way.

◉ New services like Font Squirrel have been launched, making font conversion to EOT for Internet Explorer much simpler.

◉ Type creators and type foundries are increasingly opening their licenses to Web font linking.

◉ In the short space of three months, a new font file format for the Web has been debated, a proposal has been written (WOFF), and a major browser (Firefox) has committed to implementing it.

It has been my great honor to observe and chronicle these changes and present them to you here.

However, this book is about more than just finding new typefaces to use in your designs. Another alarming trend I see in Web typography is that designers allow the default styles to set the design. Every browser comes programmed with how each element should look in the absence of design direction. Another important goal of this book is to help you understand where those defaults are, and how to think about changing them to better communicate in your own typographic voice, rather than the generic voice of the browser.

Advances in Web typography will not stop this year, and neither will the mission of this book. I have set up a new Web site—*fluidwebtype.info*—where I will be posting updates, reviews, and new techniques. At the end of each chapter, I have included a "Type Inspiration," and I will keep publishing more of those as I come across them.

I'm extremely excited by the new possibilities that are just now starting to bloom. It is my hope that this book will help designers and nondesigners alike begin to better communicate with type on the Web.

Welcome to the Web typography revolution.

— JASON CRANFORD TEAGUE
www.fluidwebtype.info
2009

Web Design is 95% Typography.

Oliver Reichenstein
Information Architects Japan

FOUNDATIONS

Letterforms should always be at the service of the message being delivered. An honest understanding of what typography can and cannot do is essential to delivering that message.

YOU ARE A TYPOGRAPHER

Whether you know it or not, if you type anything on a computer, you have committed an act of typography. You have set letterforms that will aid in the communication of a written message. You may not get ink on your thumbs or have to stress about kerning, leading, and tracking, but you have set type. Everyone is a typographer now. How good a typographer you are is up to you.

Typographer • Someone who sets written material with movable type.

Looking Glass

Georgia Italic

Typography gives text a voice

Typography is the practice of arranging type within a design. This not only includes the selection of a typeface, but also the size, spacing, color, and styles of the type. At a higher level, though, typography also deals with the design of type on the page and its interaction with other elements—such as photos, illustrations, interface chrome. This treatment of the text can be every bit as important to the message as the actual words themselves.

Everybody's voice is different, defined by tone, pitch, accents, and cadence. Typography adds a voice to text through the following:

◉ **Characters & Symbols**

Text is created by individual glyphs, each with its own unique shape and meaning. Always craft your message with the right cast of characters.

◉ **Fonts & Typefaces**

Typefaces are the skin on the bones of text. They make the first impression. Find the right fonts to speak the right message.

◉ **Scale & Rhythm**

Spacing and alignment control how the reader comprehends the text through space and time. Learn how to control the tempo of your message and guide the reader from beginning to end.

◉ **Emphasis & Contrast**

Styles determine the impact your text will have on the reader. Use styles judiciously to add highlights and counterpoints to your message without bludgeoning the reader.

◉ Grid & Composition

Layout of text in a regular sequence aids the reader's comprehension of the page. Use the grid to create order and establish hierarchy.

The Message Is Safety

Depression-era safety posters combined simple, often geo-metric imagery with strong typography to send an urgent message. Notice how the various posters combine differ-ent typefaces, colors, sizes, styles, weights, spacing, and layouts. Some of the posters shout, some ask nicely, while others speak calmly and clearly.

Finding your typographic voice

Typography gives voice to text, but in Web design much of the typography is simply left to the default values set for a particular operating system or application. Imagine if everyone spoke in the same tone of voice with no variation from one person to the next? Everyone using the same inflection and cadence monotonously? That's what we see today on the Web, not only because of the seemingly limited font family choices, but because so much is left to the defaults.

Although the type you use communicates a great deal of visual information, most people when dealing with a blank word processor page, e-mail, or blog entry tend to use whatever values the software makers have set as the default.

Content is king, so read it!

A widely accepted truism of the Web is that "content is king." Since much of the content on any given Web page will be text, then text is the king of content. This is especially true when you consider that search engines primarily look at text and its context to rank pages for relevancy.

Copy • Term used when referring to text in a layout to differentiate it from photographs or other content elements in the design.

Typography should always be at the service of the text it is presenting. To understand the type, to develop the most effective typographic voice for that text, means you must read the text.

The Web by its very nature is a dynamic medium. Keep in mind that you are often designing for content that has yet to be written.

Three Takes on a Theme

wufoo.com

squarespace.com

web-o-matic.co.nz

All three of these Web sites are meant to attract you to register for their service. Each uses typography to create a different voice for its take on the message.

A font can be many different things, depending on the context of its use—or misuse. Although seemingly a matter of semantics, it's important to understand the distinction between a font and a typeface.

The difference between typefaces and fonts

The terms *typeface* and *font* are commonly used synonymously, although they are not the same. A *typeface* is a collection of glyphs (numbers, letters, symbols, and punctuation marks) as a set. Typefaces include a number of different weights and styles. For example, Garamond is a typeface that includes italics and bold. Typefaces are also commonly referred to as *font families* or *type families*.

A *font*, on the other hand, is a collection of glyphs with one *specific* weight, style, variant, and/or stretch—for example, Garamond Bold.

In Web design, the term *font family* is used to distinguish from the more specific term *font*. The fact remains, however, that the term *font* is commonly used when *font family* or *typeface* is meant. Since the misuse is so pervasive and the distinction slightly esoteric, I'm not going to play semantics police and insist on the distinction. If it is ever critical, I'll refer to *the font* in the specific and use *typeface* or *font family* (or even *type family*) for the collection. Otherwise, assume that *font* refers to the typeface.

Looking Glass

Looking Glass

Looking Glass

Garamond (typeface)

Looking Glass

Garamond Bold (font)

Historically, *font* also referred to a particular point size of the typeface, but in the age of digital fonts—which can be scaled from a single source—this attribute is no longer relevant.

Type Designer • A person who designs typefaces.

A font is the skin on the skeleton of text

The letter "A" is represented as two diagonal lines meeting at an apex at the top with a cross line between them. A typeface adds an extra visual layer of meaning to the text beyond its simple shape. Consider the five different representations of the uppercase letter "A" below:

Each letterform, called a *glyph*, is undoubtedly the same letter, sharing the basic characteristics we have come to know as the letter "A" and communicating the same pronunciation and meaning. However, each glyph's "skin" suggests something completely different about the letter:

- **Palatino** suggests knowledge and authority.

- **Synchro LET** suggests techno or sci-fi.

- **Rosewood Std** has the look of the Old West or late 19th century.

- **Bickham Script Pro** is fluid and elegant.

- **Helvetica**, often thought of as the vanilla of fonts, takes on the voice of the design around it.

Looking Glass
Palatino

LOOKING GLASS
Synchro LET

LOOKING GLASS
Rosewood Std

Looking Glass
Bickham Script Pro

Looking Glass
Helvetica

Type classifications for Web design

Although typefaces are often roughly split into one of two groups—serif and sans serif—there are several classification systems for typefaces that further help to identify and describe them.

One classification system that you will need to know for Web typography was created by the *World Wide Web Consortium* (W3C). It was specifically created to classify typefaces for use in Cascading Style Sheets (CSS).

The CSS type classification is not extensive or terribly descriptive, is often confusing—is Courier New serif or monospace?—and deviates inexplicably from standard type classification systems—what exactly is a "fantasy" typeface, anyway?—but it's what we have and is unlikely to change.

Other classification systems may be more useful in describing type to colleagues and clients.

CSS Type Classifications

Looking Glass

Times (serif)

Looking Glass

Arial (sans serif)

Looking Glass

Courier (monospace)

Looking Glass

Snell Roundhand (cursive)

Looking Glass

Cracked (fantasy)

§ We will explore the CSS type classification system in greater detail in Chapter 3 "Fonts & Typefaces."

TYPOGRAPHY ON THE SCREEN

Web typography has grown out of the larger field of digital typography that developed with the advent and growth of the digital computer.

Going from print to screen

Originally, digital typefaces were created so that text could be output by computers to a printer, not necessarily displayed on the screen. With the rise of desktop publishing and WYSIWYG (What You See Is What You Get, pronounced wiz-e-wig) publishing, digital fonts were created that could be displayed on the computer screen as well as printed, but often required separate versions—one for printing and one for screen.

The problem is that type on the screen has a much lower clarity than printed type. Most computers have a working resolution of 72 or 96 dots per inch (dpi), while print resolution is generally 144 to 300 dpi. At lower resolutions, the subtleties of a font's design become difficult or impossible to discern.

One reason for the popularity of the font Georgia is that (in addition to being almost ubiquitously installed on computers) it was designed to look good on the screen.

Some fonts are simply better suited for viewing on the screen and some for print. To compensate for the low resolution, operating systems will *anti-alias* the text, effectively blurring the glyphs' edges to trick the eye into seeing a smooth transition between pixels on the screen. Additionally, some fonts include *hinting*—or "intelligence"—in the font outline that prevents letters in the font from becoming distorted and difficult to identify on the screen.

§ Find more information on anti-aliasing in Chapter 2, "Characters & Symbols."

Modern digital font file formats

Digital fonts are actually small pieces of computer code that work as specialized programs to tell the computer how to skin the text a particular way. Over the years, font file formats have been developed that include all of the information for both screen and print in a single file.

The first digital fonts were bitmap in nature, where the shapes were "mapped" out pixel by pixel. This meant that every font size had to be individually created, diminishing their versatility.

The next generation of fonts used vector technologies to create an outline of the basic font shape, which could then be scaled up or down to different sizes, or even used to synthesize different weights or styles.

Today, there are three digital font formats widely in use by both Mac and Windows computers:

◉ **PostScript Type 1** is an older file format that is gradually being phased out in favor of OpenType. Two files are required for Type 1 fonts, one with the actual outline information (.pfb on Windows and .lwfn on Mac), the other with metric data, such as kerning (.pfm on Windows and .fond on Mac).

◉ **TrueType** (.ttf) font files contain all of the font data in a single file. In Mac OS X you might also encounter DFONT (.dfont) files, which are TrueType files that have been converted from the older Mac OS 9 operating system.

◉ **OpenType** (.otf) is an extension of the TrueType format that includes more typographic control and allows for older Type 1 fonts to be converted.

Finding your font files

A simple fact of life in digital typography is that if users do not have access to the font file, they will not see it on their screen. This has a direct and dramatic effect on Web typography. It means whatever typeface you want to use has to be accessible to the reader's computer. There are three primary ways for this to happen:

- ◉ **Installed on the system**: Any font file that users have installed on their computer can be accessed. Where font files are stored on a computer will depend on the OS.

- ◉ **Embedded in the document**: Font information is directly embedded into a file, as in PDF and Flash files. This protects the font information from being copied and reused without permission.

- ◉ **Downloaded to the application**: The font file is downloaded and then used directly by the application. CSS has syntax that allows for downloading fonts; however, sticking points and problems can arise with supported font file formats.

In Mac OS X, font files are stored in the Library/Fonts directory and can be controlled using the Font Book application.

In Windows, font files are stored in the Windows/Fonts directory—although actual files may be anywhere—and can be controlled using the Fonts control panel.

Embedded fonts can also be included using Scalable Vector Graphics files (SVG).

Chapter 3 will explore ways to add a variety of typefaces to your Web designs, including font linking, font type services (Typekit, Kernest, and Typotheque), and other font-embedding technologies (Cufón).

A BRIEF HISTORY OF WEB TYPOGRAPHY

As design disciplines go, Web typography is extremely young and underdeveloped.

Before we can go any further, it's important to define exactly what Web typography is, since it is *not* simply the presentation of text within a browser window.

What is Web typography?

Web typography is the practice of typography applied to text marked up using HTML (Web text) and styled using CSS. Although it is commonly displayed using Web browsers, the principles of Web typography can be applied anywhere that text is rendered by HTML and CSS, such as e-mail, instant messaging, and Web-enabled widgets and applications.

What Web typography is not:

- ◉ **Text in images**: Text can be rendered in an image and will often need to be considered as part of the overall page typography design. However, because it is not true Web text and cannot be selected or edited outside of image-editing software, it is not subject to the same considerations.

- ◉ **Text in Flash**: Although Flash can be used to render text on the screen and is subject to many of the same capabilities and considerations as Web text, it is not subject to the same limitations as Web text because it's created using a proprietary software package.

First there was markup...

By the time Tim Berners-Lee conceived of the World Wide Web in the early 1990s, computer operating systems were already evolving from the command-line prompt to graphic interfaces, with type going from simple monospace fonts to more modern typefaces. The Hypertext Markup Language (HTML) included several typographic *tags* to specify paragraphs, headings, list, glossary terms, and a few other styles no longer in use.

By 1995, HTML 2.0 included tags for bold and italics, and many browsers added their own tags as well, including font and other typographic style tags. The limitations of using tags for style were quickly recognized, however—they diminish the flexibility and extensibility of documents.

The rise of CSS for Web typography

To take the burden of styling documents off of HTML, which was originally intended only as a way to specify content use, *not* appearance, in 1994 the W3C started work on a separate technology, called Cascading Style Sheets (CSS). CSS defines the appearance of content that had been marked up using HTML.

Although slow to be adopted, today CSS is considered as important as HTML in the creation of professional Web pages, in large part because of its typographic control. CSS controls font weight, font styles such as italic, text spacing, and text decoration. CSS even allows the designer to specify font families, including enabling the download of particular font files. At least in theory.

**Setting Type the
Old-Fashioned Way**

Linotype operators of the
Chicago Defender news-
paper. Chicago, Illinois.
Photograph by Russell Lee
while on assignment for
the Farm Security Adminis-
tration, April 1941.

Johannes Gutenberg invented the mechanical printing press, which automated much of the printing process, around 1450 CE. The movable type process, however, traces its roots to China 1000 years earlier, with woodblack printing, and to mid-13th-century Korea, where the first examples of movable metal type can be found.

Gutenberg's original presses used characters carved as mirror images in wood blocks, but they were later cast using more durable metal alloys. The glyphs were arranged by hand in rows to create lines of text that were then stacked with *blanks* in between lines to form pages. The pages were coated with an oil-based ink, then pressed on paper *folios* which were bound and cut into books.

The basic concepts employed by Gutenberg remained relatively unchanged well into the 19th century, when the Industrial Revolution introduced more refined ways of printing. The most advanced of these was the Linotype machine, which allowed a typesetter using a 90-character keyboard to type into place letterform molds as a "line of type" that were then used to cast the metal type as a slug used for printing.

It was not until the latter part of the 20th century when phototypesetting, the photocopier, and digital printing with the laser printer led to new innovations in the print process. The personal computer and the explosion of desktop publishing in the early 1980s led to innovation in digital type. Initially conceived to improve printing, digital typography has become increasingly important as more and more text is consumed on the screen.

Images have, obviously, been easy to download almost since the conception of the Web. Although we primarily use GIF, JPEG, and PNG formats, many browsers support EPS, TIFF, and BMP. So if images are so easy to download, what's the hang-up with fonts?

The most common digital font file formats in use today are TrueType and OpenType. If you look at your font catalog, it's likely that most of your fonts are in one of these formats, with some possibly in PostScript. However, these formats lack digital rights management (DRM), meaning that anyone can use them and share their files whether they paid for the fonts or not. It is primarily for this reason that browser manufacturers have not supported these for display in Web pages.

As an alternative, Microsoft's Internet Explorer has supported the Embedded OpenType format (.eot) for over ten years. Even so, this format is rarely seen in Web design, in part because it's an ordeal to convert existing fonts to the new format, but mostly because no other browsers could support it.

And that's where Web typography has been stalled for the last decade—you can download fonts, but common font formats have been unsupported.

The limits of Web typography

As compared with the unbridled possibilities found with typography in print and video, Web typography, as practiced outside of text in images and Flash, would seem to have some hobbling limitations:

⦿ **Limited typeface choices**: Although there are far more choices than is generally thought, it is not currently possible to choose typefaces for a design at will.

Microsoft Internet Explorer does include some filter effects, and newer versions of CSS are adding a few styles. None of these come close to what's currently possible in an application like Adobe Photoshop, though.

◉ **Limited style effects**: Unlike image editing software such as Adobe Photoshop, CSS has few type style effects to offer, only recently adding drop shadows.

◉ **Limited spacing and alignment control**: Although CSS provides text spacing, letter spacing, and line height, true letter kerning is not possible, and many of the alignment controls are nonexistent or counterintuitive.

◉ **No transformation effects**: Text can be positioned, but not rotated, skewed, scaled, or animated. These are coming, but we still have a while to wait before they are cross-browser.

Still, design is about overcoming limitations, and that's exactly what I hope to help you do in this book.

The future of Web typography

In 2009, W3C started a new Working Group, separate from the CSS Working Group, expressly to address the issue of Web fonts.

The Fonts Working Group mission is to

. . . allow wider use of fonts on the Web by identifying a font format that can be supported by all user agents, balancing font vendor concerns with the needs of authors and users and the simplicity of implementation.

From *the Fonts Work Group Charter*
(*w3.org/2009/03/fonts-wg-charter*)

Basically, they want to find a new "wrapper" for fonts that will include some form of digital rights management. Even as you read this, the debate is raging over the future of typography on the Web. If you want to enter the fray yourself, subscribe to the W3C Web Fonts Public mailing list—if you dare (*www-font-request@w3.org*).

WHAT IS
FLUID WEB TYPOGRAPHY?

Given the current limitations of Web typography and the prospects for its evolution over the next few years, it's important that Web designers be flexible in their thinking about how to design with type.

Rather than trying to hold to the absolutes guaranteed with print design, those working with type on the Web will have to find a more fluid way of working with type on the screen.

Fluid Web typography is an approach to Web typography that works within those limitations rather than trying to cover them up. Instead of working toward precise control of type on the screen, it acknowledges that in Web design,

◉ Font faces may change

◉ Font sizes may change

◉ Line lengths may change

The best strategy for dealing with these variables in design is to prepare for them and to design versatility into your designs from the outset. This will be the philosophy explored throughout this book, culminating in Chapter 6, "Grid & Composition," where I will present several best practices for fluid Web typography.

The five principles of fluid Web typography

Throughout this book, I will be stressing several key principles that will help you to create better typographic design on the Web. Some of these principles are true of typography in any medium, but take on extra significance on the Web.

Principle 1: Fluid Web typography relies on CSS for style and HTML for text.

Text is text and style is style. Once style is embedded in text, the text loses the flexibility of being easily restyled. This is true whether the HTML style tags like `<b>` for bold or `<i>` for italics are being used, or whether the styled text is embedded in an image.

The purpose of HTML is to structure the content of a page—including the text—so that CSS can be used for typography.

Principle 2: Fluid Web typography ***cannot*** be precisely controlled.

Designers want their work to look exactly the way they envisioned it, often in a more static context such as a visual comp created in a program like Photoshop. A very important reality that I often have to tell Web designers is this: *Photoshop is not the Web*.

Photoshop and other image editing software provide exacting design control within a controlled environment, where you can rely on fonts to be available and sizes to be set. All too often, designers want to replicate that precision control in the Web page. Be prepared to let go of some of that control, and plan for change. This is the hardest part of Web design, but when you get it right, your designs will begin to sing.

Principle 3: Fluid Web typography avoids using images and other kludges.

Although using text in an image will greatly increase the amount of styling that you can apply to it, text in an image is still just that—an image. It can still be read but has several inherent problems. Keep these factors in mind when deciding whether to place text in an image:

- ◉ Text should be printable at higher resolutions. Text in images will always print at 72 dpi.

- ◉ The reader should be able to select and copy text. This will obviously not be the case if the text is part of an image.

- ◉ Text should be searchable. This not only includes using a browser search to search the text on the page, but more crucially, includes the ability for search engines to find the text in your page. Although the `alt` property can compensate somewhat, it's still not the same as having the actual text on the page.

Body copy in an image?

In this page, not only is the comic book title an image, but the paragraphs of copy underneath it are as well. This makes the text unsearchable by both the user and search engines.

Principle 4: Fluid Web typography serves the content it is presenting.

No matter what the media, subject, or purpose, all typography should add to the message of the content being displayed. On the Web, though, where so much typography happens simply by default (i.e., the "typographer" does not change the default settings), typography has become monotonous and vanilla.

How do you avoid vanilla typography? Simple—leave *nothing* to default.

In this book, I will be presenting general rules and best practices for setting every typographic property at your disposal. You can also begin, as I'll show you in Chapter 6, by resetting all of the default typographic styles before you even begin work.

Do you see the difference?

The three major portals are hardly differentiated by their designs and not at all by their typography.

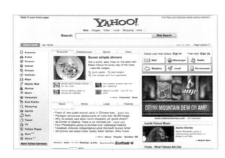

Principle 5: Fluid Web typography accommodates the reader's needs.

Anyone reading content on the Web has certain expectations about what they can and cannot do. It is your job to meet and then exceed their expectations. Meeting user expectations is easy—don't break anything that is standard practice while Web browsing. Exceeding their expectations takes more work, and means creating designs that are optimized for the end user experience based on factors like their browser, screen size, and preferences.

⊙ Although already mentioned above, it's worth repeating that one of the key reader expectations is to be able to select, copy, and paste text.

⊙ Column widths should grow or shrink to make best use of the available screen real estate, but should never grow too wide for comfortable reading.

⊙ Text should scale smoothly up or down—along with the overall page layout—in response to commands from the reader. Most modern Web browsers will handle this automatically, but there are still plenty of older browsers (such as IE6) around, and a growing audience is using mobile devices.

Type Inspirations

4AD

Typographically Innovative Music Company

4AD.com

The indie record label 4AD is renowned not only for producing some of the best artists in alternative music (the
Pixies, the Cocteau Twins, the Breeders, Tones on Tail,
Matt Johnson, to name only a very few) but also for their
incredible design aesthetic and use of typography in al-
bum cover design. The 4AD Web site carries on with that
tradition, pushing the limits of Web typography with innovative use of typeface, composition, and spacing.

How they do it:

To use specific non-Web-safe fonts, 4AD uses sIFR (discussed in Chapter 3) to replace HTML text with Flash text in many of the headlines.

Electric means of moving of information are altering our typographic culture as sharply as print modified medieval manuscript...

Marshall McLuhan
Understanding Media

CHARACTERS & SYMBOLS

Text is created by individual glyphs, each with its own unique shape and meaning. Always craft your message with the right cast of characters.

ANATOMY OF A CHARACTER

Although every character and symbol in a typeface repertoire is unique, typefaces share characteristics that we can use to describe and understand how type works.

The anatomy lesson presented in this chapter will help give you the language you need to talk about and describe different fonts as well as understand their uses and strengths. Using fonts is more than simply choosing the one that looks the best to you; it's about finding fonts that are easy to read and scan in a given situation, while also providing a visual message in line with the text.

Glyph • The visual representation of a single character or symbol within a font, distinguishable from all other characters in that set.

Looking Glass

Rockwell

The cap height, x-height, and baseline

All type is aligned to an imaginary line called the *baseline*. The baseline is generally a straight horizontal across the display surface, "breaking" to a new line as the text runs up against the right edge of the page—in Western languages, anyway. The baseline can also be angled or even curved, as needed and depending on the design of the characters.

cap height

x-height
mean line

baseline

Fonts with a larger x-height are generally easier to read on a computer screen.

§ The baseline is important when considering line height and vertical alignment, which will be discussed in Chapter 5, "Motion & Rhythm."

A font's *cap height* is the height of its tallest capital letter from the baseline. Its *x-height* is the height of the "x" glyph in that font from the baseline. The x-height is used to define the *mean line*, which runs parallel to the baseline.

The x-heights of fonts vary widely from typeface to typeface. It will be important to consider the x-height when choosing between alternate fonts in your Web design, but that's a subject for Chapter 3, "Fonts & Typefaces."

Same Letter, Many Heights

Although they are all the same letter and font size, each of these x's has a markedly different height.

times   rockwell   georgia   helvetica   monaco

Character variations within a typeface

Within a typeface you will often find many variations on the common theme of the *regular* font—called *roman* in some typefaces. The regular style is the default. It is used if no other styles are specified.

Glass *Glass*

Glass *Glass* Glass Glass   Glass

light/bold   italic/oblique   small-caps   condensed   regular

Variations include the following:

Although usable in Web typography, type weights are more limited there than in other media.

⦿ **Regular:** The upright non-bold version of the font as opposed to italic or oblique. Most typefaces refer to this as Regular, but some use Roman.

⦿ **Weight**: Many typefaces include one or more different font weights, either lighter or heavier than the default font. They generally offer bold or black for darker fonts and light or ultra light for lighter fonts.

Some fonts include versions that stretch (expanded) or contract (condensed) the font horizontally. While easily confused with weight, font stretching only affects the width of the typeface, not its thickness. Unfortunately, CSS does not currently access this property, although future versions will.

⦿ **Italics and obliques**: *Italics* refers to a unique version of the font, generally designed to look handwritten and scriptlike, and slanted to the right. While commonly confused with italics, *oblique* fonts are an angled version of the roman font, generally slanted 10° to the right.

⦿ **Small caps**: These use capital glyphs for lowercase letters, adjusting the size for contrast. Small caps are easy to synthesize for typefaces that don't include a specific version.

§ Weights, italics, obliques, and small caps are all discussed in Chapter 4, "Scale & Rhythm."

Ascenders, descenders, and other letter parts

Every character has a variety of patterns that can be described. The most important of these, at least from the standpoint of layout, are ascenders and descenders. The parts of the letter that rise above the mean line are called *ascenders*, and those that descend below the baseline are called *descenders*. How a particular font treats these will be important when finding the right font for the job, as described in Chapter 6.

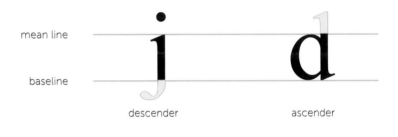

mean line

baseline

descender   ascender

You might find that the terminals in the font Modern No. 20 are too old-fashioned looking for use in a new tech-company Web site.

Looking Glass

Modern No. 20

There are several other "letter parts" that can be used to describe how letters appear. Many are holdovers from the calligraphic influences, and some are specific to a particular letter, like the spine, which only applies to "S." Although less important when actually laying out the page, these letter parts are helpful when discussing the relative strengths and weaknesses of one font over another for a particular design.

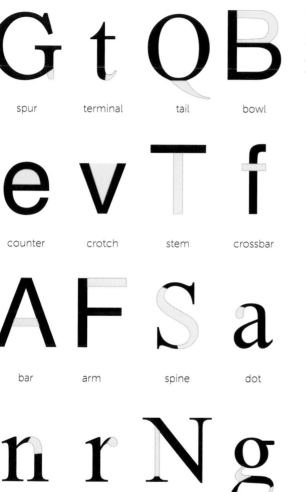

spur terminal tail bowl

counter crotch stem crossbar

bar arm spine dot

shoulder ear hairline link & loop

Letter Parts

Like people, every character is different. Like human
anatomy, common traits
can be described.

TYPES OF TYPE

Although type can come in virtually any shape, fonts fall into certain classes, depending on their characteristics. To talk intelligently about typefaces, you need to know what these general classifications are.

Monospace or proportional typefaces

Monospace—or *fixed-width*—characters occupy the exact same horizontal space, and the space between each letter does not vary. Alternatively, *proportional*—or *variable-width*—fonts occupy as much horizontal space as is needed to display the glyph, as set by the typographer, and the amount of space between glyphs will vary as needed for optimal legibility.

monospace Looking Glass

proportional Looking Glass

Monospace fonts were originally developed for typewriters, which required consistency between each letter. They are often used to display computer code, where consistent type sizes are helpful for debugging. However, monospaced types are less legible than proportional types are for body copy, and even less legible at larger sizes.

Serifed or sans-serif typefaces

A serif is a small flourish at the end of a character. The stroke is flared out in an attempt to improve legibility—especially at smaller sizes in print—by helping the eye differentiate one character from the next, and to add typographic texture. Sans-serif fonts avoid the use of flourishes in favor of straighter lines and simpler curves.

⌇ Choosing between serifed and sans-serif fonts is discussed in Chapter 6, "Grid & Composition."

serif   sans-serif

In print, serifs improve legibility by adding more visual contrast between glyphs. However, on screens and especially at smaller sizes (12px or below), serifs tend to blur the letter, making them less distinct and less legible.

Although generally thought of as a single group, serifs vary widely and are categorized in three main serif classes:

◉ **Bracketed serifs** are the most common. These serifs are smoothly curved flourishes emerging from the letter in a form called a *fillet*.

◉ **Unbracketed serifs** meet the letterform at sharper angles, giving the font a more geometric appearance.

◉ **Slab serifs** have rectangular serifs with a uniform thickness and squared corners, making them popular for monospace fonts.

bracketed serif

unbracketed serif

M

slab serif

Defining type roles: Text, display, and decorative type

The most useful way that we can classify typefaces is by their general use in the design. Type is broken into three groups—text, display, and decorative.

◉ **Text**: Typefaces that are used to display large amounts of body copy need to be as easy to read as possible. A legible font is easy on the eyes for the long stretch. For the screen, this generally means sans-serif fonts, with the exception of serifed fonts like Georgia that were designed as text fonts for the screen. Franklin Gothic Book, seen on the left, is an example of a strong sans-serif text font.

◉ **Display**: Headline and other larger copy use display fonts that are more eye-catching to attract the reader's attention. Although what catches the eye can be a matter of taste, these fonts are generally bolder and wider than text fonts. Cooper Black is a strong thick font that will stand out in headlines.

◉ **Decorative**: In addition to the easily classifiable types of characters, there are those that are more free form and don't easily fit into any particular group, like Mistral. These are generally referred to as decorative type. In CSS, they are referred to as *fantasy* or *cursive*. They rarely make good text fonts but can be good at larger sizes or for headlines.

Looking Glass

Franklin Gothic Book

Looking Glass

Cooper Black

Looking Glass

Mistral

Dingbats and other nonalphabetic type

Although most fonts contain alphanumeric glyphs, many also contain punctuation and other important marks and symbols. In addition, some fonts contain pictograms called *dingbats*, and some fonts may be nothing but dingbat characters—with no letters at all. Known as *pi fonts*, these can literally contain anything and are generally specialized for a specific purpose, such as mathematics, cartography, or other disciplines with their own symbols.

Unfortunately, these typefaces are not very useful in Web typography. There are very few Web-safe pi fonts, and many of these (like Webdings) will not display in Web browsers like Firefox. Unless you can be certain that the font is available, the glyph you've chosen will be replaced by a corresponding character in the default non-pi font.

§ Later in this chapter, you will find out how to add a variety of different pictogram characters without having to use a dingbat font.

Webdings

The font Webdings is a common dingbat font installed on most computers. However, some browsers—such as Firefox and Opera—do not display it, rendering it all but useless.

FAKING HIGHER RESOLUTION WITH ANTI-ALIASED TEXT

aliased text

anti-aliased text

As mentioned in Chapter 1, "Foundations," the screen has a substantially lower resolution than the printed page. A computer screen is composed of a series of tiny squares (pixels) that combine to make everything from a photograph to a letter. While print has a resolution of 144 dpi (dots per inch) or higher (usually at least 300 dpi for high-quality printing) computer screens have a resolution between 72 dpi and 96 dpi. This lower resolution means that characters on the computer screen tend to look rough and blocky, with the pixels evident to the naked eye.

To compensate and increase legibility and readability of text, most operating systems use a process called *anti-aliasing*, which adds transparent pixels to the edges of letters, producing the optical illusion that the edges of the text are smooth.

On the Mac, anti-aliasing is called *text smoothing* and is controlled in the Appearance control panel. In Windows, the technology is called *ClearType* and is controlled in the Display Control Panel. While font smoothing is turned on by default on the Mac, it was not in Windows until Vista. Anti-aliasing cannot be controlled by the Web designer.

CHARACTER AND TEXT ENCODING ON THE WEB

To a computer, a character is nothing more than a bit of code that it recognizes to display a particular glyph on a screen (or print, or other output media). The shapes of letters, numbers, and other symbols are meaningless to the computer; it only know the code to display a particular glyph so that humans can understand it.

Character encoding or *font encoding* is a system that pairs each character in a given font with the computer code needed to display it. On the flip side, with *text encoding,* all of the text in any document is encoded by the computer, each letter having its own unique code "number."

There are a number of different standards that can be used to encode a computer file such as a font or text document. Like trying to understand a different human language, if a computer doesn't understand a particular encoding "language"—or know which encoding system is being used—the text is likely to appear as gibberish.

As long as the computer program displaying the text understands the encoding used by the font and the encoding used by the text document—and all the glyphs needed are included in the font—then the text will display just as you wrote it. Even if the font and text file are encoded differently, the program will translate between them.

The Web has begun to standardize around a common encoding language called Unicode. If you stick to it, you are unlikely to have problems with gibberish text.

Check your font's character set to make sure that it has everything you need

A *character set* is simply that—the set of all characters in a particular font in a particular order for its particular encoding scheme. This is referred to as the font *repertoire* or *character range*; every glyph is in order for the encoding scheme, which is why the term *character set* is often used synonymously with *character encoding*.

A font's character set does not necessarily include every possible character that can be encoded. Some fonts even include alternatives to the expected character. This is, in fact, how a dingbat font works—each letter space contains the information used to display the dingbat glyph rather than a letter.

Gill Sans Character Set

Although it contains all of the usual suspects—A–Z, a–z, and 0–9—the complete character set for Gill Sans (designed by Eric Gill) not only contains an assortment of common punctuation marks, symbols, and other marks; many fonts will also include characters used by languages other than English.

When designing for the Web, you must be sure that the fonts you choose contain all of the characters you need to display your text. If a font does not include a particular character in its repertoire, the result will depend on how the particular application handles nonexistent characters, but will not be the result you want. Generally, a placeholder glyph will be used, such as a rectangle with an "x" or a diamond with a "?" inside or just empty space.

Barrett Ironwork Character Set

Including uppercase styles for both upper- and lowercase glyphs as well as several dingbats, the character set for Barrett Ironwork has a more limited repertoire than Gill Sans.

If a particular character is not available in the font's character set, it will generally be replaced with a rectangle.

Missing characters are rarely a problem with English, since most common fonts include a full repertoire of 26 English alphabetic characters in both upper- and lowercase, along with common punctuation. In fact, most professionally created fonts include the entire Latin character set used to display Western languages. It's generally the more specialized and decorative fonts that will give you problems.

Bad Character Encoding

In the example to the left, a special separator character is not available in the repertoire of the font being used to display the message and is replaced by a diamond shape with a question mark inside.

Child Safety ◆ Follow-up on False Alarm (but read #5)

Know your encoding: Unicode vs. ISO Latin-1

Literally hundreds of different character encoding systems have been developed over the years, most famously ASCII (American Standard Code for Information Interchange), Mac OS Roman (used in older versions of the Macintosh operating system), and multiple Windows encoding systems for different languages. Most are defined as either Western or non-Western, depending on the glyphs needed to display particular languages.

For the Web, the most common encoding system is the Unicode format. Unicode is considered superior to other encoding methods because its repertoire includes over 100,000 possible characters from a variety of languages. A font using Unicode can contain a complete character set for multiple languages in a single font file, although it probably won't. Fonts for specific languages are more likely to give results that are acceptable to native speakers than fonts that try to cover many languages and scripts.

The most common Unicode format in use today is UTF-8. The *8* refers to how many bits are used to store each letter, meaning that a UTF-8 encoded file can contain a maximum of 256 individual character glyphs.

The newer UTF-16 is capable of encoding the entire Unicode repertoire of characters in a single file, but it is not supported by all Web browsers for text encoding.

An older alternative for Western language encoding that you might still run into on the Web is ISO 8859-1 (or ISO Latin 1). Similar to UTF-8, it also uses 8 bits to store characters.

Most text editors and Web editing software allow you to switch your file encoding, but I wouldn't. If you do start to see the wrong characters being displayed, it's likely due to inconsistent encoding. My advice is to set them to UTF-8 and then walk away.

Setting a Web page's encoding

Although there are a wide variety of ways to encode a text file—HTML, CSS, and JavaScript files are all text files—encoding is only rarely an issue on the Web because most browsers automatically recognize the file's encoding type and adjust accordingly. For the most part, character encoding happens automatically, and you will not need to change settings.

One place you will always need to specify the encoding being used is directly in the HTML of your document. To make sure the browser knows which encoding system you are using, in the head of your HTML, add the following line of code if you are using UTF-8:

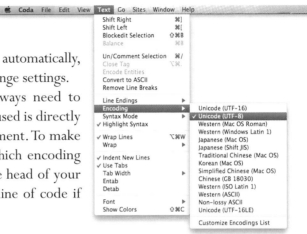

```
<meta http-equiv="Content-Type"
      content="text/html;charset=utf-8">
```

If you are using ISO Latin 1, the code is
If you are using another encoding system, then

```
<meta http-equiv="Content-Type"
    content="text/html;
    charset=iso-8859-1">
```

Choosing Your Text File's Encoding

Web code editing software like Coda (panic.com) allows you to switch your file encoding. Unless you are setting your encoding for a specific language, it's best to leave it set for UTF-8.

you will need to replace the charset value with the appropriate encoding value. As long as the charset is defined, the browser will be able to associate the right character with the right glyph in your chosen font.

USING SYMBOLS

While alphanumeric characters will likely make up the bulk of your text, it is important to consider all of the different typographic marks at your disposal. Content creators are often confounded when trying to use characters that do not appear directly on the keyboard. However, it is the richness of these characters that can really set your typographic design apart.

Many characters are "hidden" behind the Shift, Control, and Option keys. Operating systems include character map software that lets you view the entire character set of a font, with options for inserting glyphs into documents.

Generally, if you are using proper encoding (UTF-8 is the safest) and your font has the correct glyph as a part of its character set, any character you can type or insert will be displayed in your Web page. This is obviously not the case if you are using a dingbat font or a font intended for a language other than the one you are using.

Character Viewer

Mac (below), Windows (next page), and Unix (not shown) operating systems all include some form of character viewer application that lets you view and place any of the glyphs available in a font's repertoire.

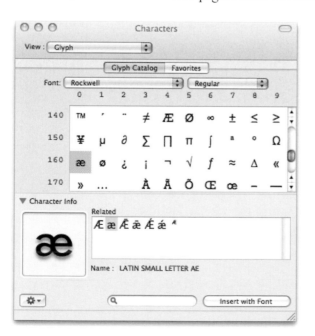

Adding symbols to HTML code

There are many characters that can be included in an HTML file by typing a name value between an ampersand and a semicolon—for example, `&mdash;` for an em dash (—). Officially known as the *character entity references*, they are more commonly referred to as *HTML characters* or *ampersand characters*.

The advantage of using HTML characters as opposed to typing the character directly into your HTML code is that these references are displayed independently of the document's text encoding, and so should work in any HTML file regardless of the character encoding.

As always, the font you choose will still contain the character you want in its set, but this is one way to avoid problems where special characters might get confused if the wrong encoding is used.

The next two pages show a list of some of the most common entities, and Appendix B, "Glossary of Characters," has all of the HTML entities as well as UTF character entities to add even more glyphs.

HTML CHARACTER REFERENCES

To ensure that a special character is properly encoded in your HTML, you will want to use its name or number character reference rather than typing the glyph in directly. This table presents some of the most common glyphs you will need. For a full list of all available characters and values, see Appendix B, "Glossary of Characters."

Name	Character	Description
†	†	dagger
•	•	bullet, black small circle
…	…	horizontal ellipsis, three dot leader
‰	‰	per mill sign
‹	‹	single left-pointing angle quote
›	›	single right-pointing angle quote
♠	♠	black spade suit
♣	♣	black club suit
♥	♥	black heart suit
♦	♦	black diamond suit
‾	‾	overline
←	←	leftward arrow
↑	↑	upward arrow
→	→	rightward arrow
↓	↓	downward arrow
™	™	trademark sign
"	"	double straight quotation mark
'	'	apostrophe/single straight quotation mark
&	&	ampersand
–	–	en dash
—	—	em dash

Name	Character	Description
		nonbreaking space
¡	¡	inverted exclamation
¢	¢	cent sign
£	£	pound sterling
¤	¤	general currency sign
¥	¥	yen sign
¦	¦	broken vertical bar
§	§	section sign
©	©	copyright
«	«	left angle quote
¬	¬	not sign
®	®	registered trademark
¯	¯	macron accent
°	°	degree sign
±	±	plus or minus
¹	¹	superscript one
²	²	superscript two
³	³	superscript three
´	´	acute accent
µ	µ	micro sign
¶	¶	paragraph sign
·	·	middle dot
»	»	right angle quote
¼	¼	one-fourth
½	½	one-half
¾	¾	three-fourths
×	×	multiplication sign
Ø	Ø	uppercase O, slash
÷	÷	division sign

Choose the right symbol for the job

Because of the limited nature of early Web typography and—to be honest—the lack of training of many of the people creating content for the Web, many characters were misused or misunderstood. Sometimes this was fine; however, sometimes disaster ensued.

Now that you know where to find all of the characters and how to replace them with HTML encoded character references, there's no excuse for using the wrong character. If you need to see the full rules for character use, I recommend *The Elements of Style*, by William Strunk Jr. But I want to offer a few suggestions for the use of special characters in the Web here.

Multiplication

multiplication symbol

X

lowercase "x"

The multiplication symbol looks a lot like a lowercase "x," but they are not the same. Many content creators will use a lowercase "x" or an asterisk (*) instead of ×. Typographically, they look and work differently, especially in proportional and serifed fonts.

Use `&times;` when you want to place a multiplication symbol in your page.

Fractions

1/2   1/4   3/4

fractions with slash

½   ¼   ¾

fraction glyphs

Although commonly expressed as a simple ratio using a slash character (for example, 1/2), typographically, fractions are meant to be styled with smaller numerals kerned closely together (for example, ½). The three most common fractions are included as HTML characters and should be used where possible.

Use `&frac14;`, `&frac12;`, and `&frac34;`.

Displaying HTML code in HTML code

Most parentheses and brackets appear as typed. One exception is the less than (<) and greater than (>) signs, called *chevrons*, used to create the actual HTML code. Additionally, use straight quotes in code, and always encode them when in text to avoid having the browser interpret the display code as actual code.

To display HTML code on your Web page, you will need to encode it using `&lt;` and `&gt;`. For quotes use `&quot;` or `&apos.`

Link arrows

Using the right double angled quote or right arrow as a typographic flourish to indicate that a block of text is a hypertext link has become somewhat of a Web standard.

Many content creators, not knowing how to create the appropriate character, have opted to use two greater-than signs instead, which not only take up a lot more space, but are simply not as attractive.

Use `&raquo;` or `&rarr;` when you want an arrow for a link.

right angle quote

right arrow

two chevrons

Ellipses

Ellipses appear as three consecutive dots used to indicate the omission of a word or phrase in a sentence. Ellipses are also often used to represent the interruption, pause, or trailing off of a statement in mid-speech.

Although an ellipsis looks a lot like three periods, it is not the same thing, and periods should not be substituted.

Use `&hellip;`.

ellipses

three periods

Smart quotes, part 1

One place where a special character should *not* be used is in code. Smart quotes in any code will break the code, often causing the code to display as text.

Always use straight quotes for code.

Smart quotes, part 2

double and single
smart quotes

double and single
straight quotes

What word processors refer to as *smart*—also called *curved* and *book*—quotes should be used for any formal writing. Generally, quotes are typed with the keyboard, appearing as straight quotes in the code, but rendered as smart quotes by the browser. As mentioned above, though, straight quotes—also called *typewriter* quotes—should only be used when representing computer code.

To ensure that the proper quotation mark is used, it's a good idea to encode smart quotes and apostrophes with `&ldquo;` and `&rdquo;` for double quotes, and with `&lsquo;` and `&rsquo;` for single quotes and apostrophes.

Hyphens vs. minuses vs. dashes

hyphen

minus

en dash

em dash

Hyphens are easily inserted from the keyboard, but are often used when a minus sign, an en dash, or an em dash is what is called for. In typography, the hyphen should be used only to hyphenate words.

Minus signs are longer, and used in mathematics to indicate subtraction ($1-1=0$). Use `&minus;`.

An en dash is the same width as the minus sign but is generally thinner and should be used for date ranges (4 March–6 March). Use `&ndash;`.

An em dash is used to separate a parenthetical—like this. Use `&mdash;`.

Spaces

Although the basic space is fine for most uses, there are a number of spaces that can be encoded to achieve various widths or to prevent breaking between words.

Use   for a nonbreaking space.

Use ace; or ace; for spaces the same width as an en dash or em dash.

Use   for a space 20% of an em dash.

Feet and inches

Although generally single (') and double (") quotes are used for feet and inches, respectively, the actual symbols are the prime (′) and double prime (″), which look more like straight quotes slanted to the right.

Use ′ for single prime and ″ (capital "P") for double prime.

Logograms

A logogram is a symbol that represents a word, such as the ampersand (&), but also includes registered trademark (®), trademark (™), and copyright symbols (©).

As these symbols are often critical for legal reasons, add them using HTML character references to ensure that they will display correctly regardless of encoding.

Use & for ampersand, ® for registered trademark, ™ for trademark, and © for copyright.

5'11"

quotes

5'11″

primes

&

ampersand

®™©

registered trademark,
trademark, and copyright

Type Inspirations

Poems Out Loud

Great poetry deserves great type.

poemsoutloud.net

Started in 2009, Poems Out Loud features columns and recorded readings by well-known and award-winning poets as well as general poetry news and ephemera. The name of the site was inspired by the anthology edited by Robert Pinsky called *Essential Pleasures: A New Anthology of Poems to Read Aloud*.

Their Web site uses a variety of typefaces and typographic weights and styles to create bold but easy-to-read Web content.

How they do it:

POL uses Cufón (explained in Chapter 3) to download JavaScript versions of the fonts Facebuster 400 and Helvetica Neue Thin Condensed, combining these with the Web safe font Baskerville to create a compelling typographic texture.

poems out **LOUD**

audio video columns
newsletter about subscribe

search go

Zac Efron Dives for Dreams

By **THE EDITORS** on 9.03.09

Universal Pictures has purchased the right to use one of the many poems by e. e. cummings that I consider nothing-if-not-fodder-for-motivational-speakers entitled "Dive for Dreams." The poem will be featured in the upcoming film *The Death and Life of Charlie St. Cloud*. Gladly, neither Jennifer Aniston nor Aaron Eckhart will get anywhere near it, as *St. Cloud* stars Zac Efron and Kim Basinger. "Diving for Dreams" is collected in *95 Poems*, originally published in 1950, it was the last book of Cummings's new poems to be published during his lifetime.

continue reading » comments (0)

Video: Charlie Smith at Bryant Park

By **THE EDITORS** on 9.02.09

In January 2009, New York-based poet Charlie Smith published his seventh poetry collection, *Word Comix*. But in July, at Bryant Park, Smith read from what he jokingly referred to as a "lighter book" published in 2000 called *Heroin*. Lorrie Moore, author of the much anticipated new novel *A Gate at the Stairs*, described *Heroin* as "appallingly brilliant."

continue reading » comments (0)

A Design Against Darkness
Poetry for Troubled Times

By **KIM ADDONIZIO** on 9.02.09

Sometimes the world seems to me utterly random, possibly malevolent, and therefore frightening. I always go back to Robert Frost's sonnet, "Design" which closes, "*What but design of darkness to appall?—/ If design govern in a thing so small.*"

When I read this poem, I end up feeling oddly comforted. Someone else was asking the same questions, feeling the chill, getting it down in language. Someone was fashioning a poem. A design against darkness.

continue reading » comments (1)

Memoir and Poetry

By **HONOR MOORE** on 8.28.09

Back in the mid-eighties I wrote a poem called "Memoir" for a friend who had died of AIDS. It seemed the perfect title for an elegiac poem that combined memory with dream and imaginative vision, so much so that I took it for the title of my first book of poems. When *Memoir*, a collection that drew on love, dream, memory, and family, was published in 1988, the title was seen as evocative and original. Memoir was an obscure genre—the earliest I remember reading was Maxine Hong Kingston's *The Woman Warrior*, in which the author's prose was poetic and metaphorical and in which her narrative drew on myth and cultural history as well as autobiographical incident.

continue reading » comments (4)

American Hybrid
From Anthology to Conversation

By **COLE SWENSEN** and **DAVID ST. JOHN** on 8.26.09

By way of introduction, we are the editors of a poetry anthology called *American Hybrid*. A poetry anthology is an implicit conversation about poetics, about history, about the role of the arts in society, but the conversation just starts there. We'd like to use this Poems Out Loud column to let that conversation overflow into the literal, where American poetry can be discussed in its widest sense, its current state and its future.

continue reading » comments (0)

FEATURED *Columns*
see all »

Completely Political
By Gerald Stern

A Design Against Darkness
By Kim Addonizio

Notes on the First Person
By April Bernard

Recommended **LISTENING**
see all »

B. H. Fairchild reads *Frieda Pushnik*
listen ◄»

David Baker reads *Too Many*
listen ◄»

Kim Addonizio reads *You Were*
listen ◄»

SIGN UP *for the* POETRY NEWSLETTER

email address go

FOLLOW US *on twitter*
twitter.com/poemsoutloud

SUBSCRIBE *in iTunes*
go to iTunes

TOPICS
News / Interviews / Columnist / Featured Columns / Essential Pleasures /

Robert Frost, Speaking on Campus: Excerpts from His Talks 1949-1962
The Never Before Published Lectures of America's Master-Poet

TYPE DESIGN IS AN ACT OF PLAGIARISM IN ITSELF—YOU BASICALLY RECREATE THE FLESH OF THE SAME SKELETON.

Alejandro Lo Celso Saravia

Step Inside Design, May | June 2008

FONTS & TYPEFACES

Typefaces are the skin on the bones of text, but that skin is the cover that makes a first impression. Find the right fonts to speak the right message.

FONTS ON THE WEB

When most people think of typography, they immediately think of fonts (or typefaces, to be technical). When they think of typography on the Web, they immediately think of Arial, Times, and Georgia. If they are really in the know, they may even think about Verdana and Trebuchet MS. There is no escaping that, as it stands now, the number of fonts used on the Web is staggeringly few. By the end of this chapter, though, I hope to have shown you that you have a lot more choices. Although still more limited than in print or video, there are many more than the core Web fonts for you to choose from.

Font Sub-setting • A way to reduce a font file's size for use on the Web is to sub-set it, removing all glyphs that are not being used on the page.

LOOKING GLASS

NoMak

Web typography = limited font choices?

The best estimates that I can find place the total number of computer fonts available at over 100,000. Yet, looking at Web design, you would never know there were so many choices. By and large, a subset of only five fonts are regularly used, with three of those comprising the lion's share of all type on the Web.

Although typography is about more than just choosing a typeface, it is the best place to start and the most noticeable way to differentiate your design from others'. But if everybody looks the same, then no one has to worry, right?

Quick story: I briefly worked at IBM in the mid-1990s. There I met lifetime company employees who were having a hard time adjusting to many of the changes being made in the corporation. The most difficult challenge they had, though, was with the dress code, which had been changed to business casual (slacks and polos) from business formal (suits and ties).

100,000

number of fonts available

5

number of fonts regularly
used on the Web

**The Five Fonts Everybody
Uses Today**

Looking Glass

Times

Looking Glass

Arial

Looking Glass

Georgia

Looking Glass

Verdana

Looking Glass

Trebuchet MS

I remember a 40-year veteran of IBM telling me how he hated the new dress code because he now had too many choices. When it was suits and ties, he just reached into his closet, pulled out his outfit of the day, and was done. Now he had to consider whether the colors and patterns matched. He had to actually *think* about what he was wearing.

I believe that a lot of Web content producers, developers, and, yes, even designers suffer from the same mind-set as my friend—having a limited font palette is a great excuse for not having to think about the fonts you use in your designs. But that excuse is about to evaporate like mist on a sunny morning. Get ready to put on your thinking cap.

In this chapter, you will learn about four different methods for adding typefaces to Web pages, each with its own strengths and weaknesses:

Font Foundries

emigre.com

Font foundries, like Emigre, create dozens of beautiful high-quality fonts, but they are only usable on the Web if included in an image. To protect their work, they place restrictions on their use for embedding in electronic documents such as Web pages.

- ◉ **Web safe fonts**: Fonts that are likely to be preinstalled on the end user's machine beyond the ten core Web fonts.

- ◉ **Linked Web fonts**: Fonts that are downloaded from your server to the end user's machine much like image files.

- ◉ **Web font service bureaus**: Fonts that are downloaded from a third party to the end user's machine.

- ◉ **Web font embedding technologies**: Characters are replaced by glyphs from a particular font using JavaScript.

CSS Generic Font Families

Looking Glass

serif (Times)

Looking Glass

sans-serif (Arial)

`Looking Glass`

monospace (Courier)

Looking Glass

cursive (Snell Round-
hand)

Looking Glass

fantasy (Cracked)

CSS font family classifications

As discussed in Chapter 1, "Foundations," there are a number of systems for classifying fonts. The one that is most relevant to Web typography was created by the W3C to classify font families for use in CSS. This *CSS font families* classification system is also known as the *generic font family*. It includes the following:

◉ **serif**: Fonts with serifs (see Chapter 2, "Characters & Symbols"), like Times, Georgia, Garamond, Perpetua, and Rockwell.

◉ **sans-serif**: Fonts that are not serifed, including Helvetica, Arial, Century Gothic, and Lucida Sans.

◉ **monospace**: Fonts where each glyph has the same width and spacing, including Courier, Courier New, and Andale Mono.

◉ **cursive**: Fonts that attempt to mimic human handwriting or script, including Snell Roundhand, Bradley Hand ITC TT, Brush Script MT, and Lucida Calligraphy.

◉ **fantasy**: Fonts that don't easily fit categorization, including Cracked, Curlz MT, and Bauhaus 93.

The CSS font family classifications are intended to help a Web browser identify the type of font you are *trying* to use in your design. For example, if you are using the font Arial, then you would define the generic font family as `sans-serif`. If Arial is not available, then another sans-serif font will be substituted.

Specifying typefaces with CSS

Defining the font to be used by text on a Web page is done with CSS using the `font` or `font-family` property:

```
font: bold italic normal 12px/1.5 helvetica, arial, sans-serif;
font-family: helvetica, arial, sans-serif;
```

The `font-family` property allows you to set the typeface, while the `font` property is a shortcut that lets you set not only the typeface, but also the font weight (bold), font style (italic), font variant (small caps), font size, and line height, all in a single line.

The list of typefaces is the *font-stack*, with each subsequent typeface name tried in order until a match is found on the user's computer. If the browser does not have access to the first font (Helvetica, for example)—because either the font is not installed on the user's computer or it has not been downloaded—then the next font (Arial) is tried as a fallback, and so on until all of the fonts in the list are exhausted.

§ The best practices for creating a font-stack are explored in Chapter 6, "Grid & Composition."

Name the Font!

Need to identify a typeface in a hurry? MyFonts.com provides a handy little iPhone app called WhatTheFont that analyzes text in a photo, then identifies or delivers a list of similar fonts.

WEB SAFE FONTS

The fundamental fact of Web typography is that if a font is not available to the end user's Web browser, then it will not appear when the user views your Web page. Fonts that are readily accessible on the end's machine are referred to as *Web safe fonts*. It does not matter how many fonts you have at your disposal on *your* computer—if people viewing your Web page do not have that font file on their computer or the browser cannot somehow download it, they will not see the Web design the way you do.

This is why so many Web sites use the same fonts. They rely on the nine core Web fonts that are almost ubiquitously available on computers around the world.

However, almost all computers have more than nine fonts installed on them. This is where we will begin looking to improve our selection of typefaces.

Core Web safe fonts

In 1996, recognizing that a standard set of fonts would need to be available to Web site producers, the Microsoft Corporation started the TrueType Core Fonts for the Web project. Their goal was to create a standard pack of fonts for the Internet that would

◉ Be optimal for screen legibility

◉ Offer as wide a range of variation as possible within a small set of fonts

◉ Allow extensive internationalization by including fonts with multilanguage encoding

Originally, ten fonts were selected, licensed by Microsoft, and distributed widely with a number of browsers and operating systems including Windows and Mac. Andale Mono has since been removed from Windows but is still included on the Mac.

The TrueType Core Fonts for the Web project ended in 2002 with Microsoft protesting that the fonts were being distributed by third parties in violation of the End User License Agreement (EULA). Still, most of the fonts from the original project are still distributed with current versions of Windows (with the exception of Andale Mono) and Mac OS X. Given that between them these operating systems make up about 96% of the market, it's a fair bet that any computer you are sending content to will have these fonts. The absence of a more reliable alternative explains why these typefaces still dominate Web typography today.

Although not inherently bad fonts, the very fact that they are the *only* fonts commonly used in Web designs has led to an inevitable backlash against their monotony.

TrueType Core Fonts for the Web

The TrueType Core Fonts for the Web project was shut down April 12, 2002.

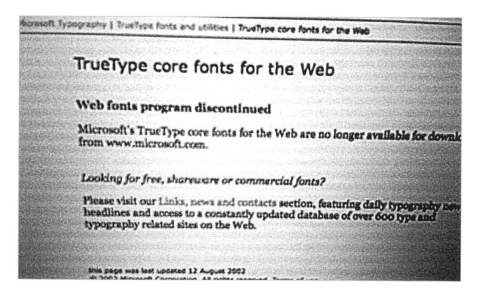

Arial

ABCDEFGHIJKLMNOPQRSTUVWXYZ
abcdefghijklmnopqrstuvwxyz
0123456789

bold, *italic*, ***bold italic***

Times New Roman

ABCDEFGHIJKLMNOPQRSTUVWXYZ
abcdefghijklmnopqrstuvwxyz
0123456789

bold, *italic*, ***bold italic***

Georgia

ABCDEFGHIJKLMNOPQRSTUVWXYZ
abcdefghijklmnopqrstuvwxyz
0123456789

bold, *italic*, ***bold italic***

Ikea, the Swedish furniture manufacturer, recently switched the font used in its iconic instructions from the elegant Futura to the less-than-elegant Verdana, much to the distress of many typographers.

Verdana

ABCDEFGHIJKLMNOPQRSTUVWXYZ
abcdefghijklmnopqrstuvwxyz
0123456789

bold, *italic*, ***bold italic***

Trebuchet MS

ABCDEFGHIJKLMNOPQRSTUVWXYZ
abcdefghijklmnopqrstuvwxyz
0123456789

bold, *italic*, ***bold italic***

Andale Mono

ABCDEFGHIJKLMNOPQRSTUVWXYZ
abcdefghijklmnopqrstuvwxyz
0123456789

Courier New

ABCDEFGHIJKLMNOPQRSTUVWXYZ
abcdefghijklmnopqrstuvwxyz
0123456789

bold, *italic*, ***bold italic***

Comic Sans MS

ABCDEFGHIJKLMNOPQRSTUVWXYZ
abcdefghijklmnopqrstuvwxyz
0123456789

bold

Impact

ABCDEFGHIJKLMNOPQRSTUVWXYZ
abcdefghijklmnopqrstuvwxyz
0123456789

Webdings

The Core Web Fonts

The original ten Web fonts. Andale Mono is still included with Mac OS, but is no longer included with Windows.

All of the fonts, except Webdings, of course, are encoded with standard Western and Cyrillic glyphs.

By default, Webdings will not be recognized in Opera or in Firefox, unless you are willing to change settings in their code.

§ For a complete list of all Web safe fonts with samples, styles, and weights, see Appendix D, "Web Font Specimen Book."

number of fonts added with Windows XP

number of fonts added with Windows Vista

115

number of fonts added with MS Office for Windows

OS Web safe fonts

The core Web fonts have the advantage of being pre-installed on computers almost ubiquitously, but these are not the only fonts that the operating systems pre-install. Remember, the only limitation on the fonts you choose is that the end user's computer must be able to access them, and both the Mac and Windows operating systems pre-install more than the ten core Web fonts.

Pre-installed Windows fonts

On Windows, the best sources of pre-installed fonts are the operating system itself and Microsoft Office, which is likely also pre-installed.

⦿ **Windows XP** adds nine mostly excellent fonts, including sans-serif alternatives like Franklin Gothic Medium, Lucida Sans Unicode, and Tahoma, and the wedge serif font Palatino. Marlett is also included, but it is only a placeholder font used in interfaces and of limited use.

⦿ **Windows Vista** adds another seven fonts to the nine already included in Windows XP. All but one of these inexplicably begin with the letter "C."

⦿ **Microsoft Office**: 2003 includes 110 fonts, and Office 2007 adds five on top of that.

In total, this gives Windows users a possible 131 fonts above and beyond the core Web fonts.

Pre-installed Mac fonts

The Mac operating system installs several fonts in addition to the core Web fonts, and even more with iLife, which is standard on all Macs. Additionally, many Mac users install the Mac version of MS Office or Apple iWork.

- **Mac OS X** includes 30 text display and decorative fonts.

- **iLife '09** is pre-installed on all Macs, with iWeb, iPhoto, GarageBand, iDVD, and iMovie. It adds another 13 fonts, primarily display and decorative, but also including Palatino, a serifed font similar to Palatino Linotype, which is installed by the Windows operating system.

- **iWork '09** is a popular, but by no means ubiquitous, application suite for the Mac that include Pages, Keynote, and Numbers as well as 25 additional fonts, although ten of these are also installed with iLife.

- **MS Office for Mac 2008** installs 72 fonts, many of which are also installed by Microsoft Office for Windows.

Adjusting for overlap, this adds 125 fonts that are guaranteed or likely to be available to Mac users viewing your Web designs.

30

number of fonts added
with Mac OS X

13

number of fonts added
with Apple iLife '09

72

number of fonts added
with MS Office: Mac 2008

25

number of fonts added
with Apple iWork '09

FONTS & TYPEFACES

Windows XP +9

Franklin Gothic Medium

Lucida Console

Lucida Sans Unicode

Marlett

Microsoft Sans Serif

Palatino Linotype

Symbol

Tahoma

Wingdings

Windows Vista +16

Windows XP fonts +

Calibri

Cambria

Candara

Consolas

Constantia

Corbel

Segoe UI

MS Office +115
(bold Office 2007 only)

Agency FB

Algerian

Arial Narrow

Arial Rounded MT

Arial Unicode MS

Baskerville Old Face

Bauhaus 93

Bell MT

Berlin Sans FB

Berlin Sans FB Demi Bold

Bernard MT Condensed

Blackadder ITC

Bodoni MT

Bodoni MT Condensed

Bodoni MT Poster
Compressed

Book Antiqua

Bookman Old Style

Bookshelf Symbol 7

Bradley Hand ITC

Britannic Bold

Broadway

Brush Script MT

Californian FB

Calisto MT

Cambria Math

Castellar

Centaur

Century

Century Gothic

Century Schoolbook

Chiller

Colonna MT

Cooper Black

Copperplate Gothic Bold

Copperplate Gothic Light

Curlz MT

Edwardian Script ITC

Elephant

Engravers MT

Eras Bold ITC

Eras Demi ITC

Eras Light ITC

Eras Medium ITC

Felix Titling

Footlight MT Light

Forte

Franklin Gothic Book

Freestyle Script

French Script MT

Garamond

Gigi

Gill Sans MT

Gill Sans Ultra Bold

Goudy Old Style

Gloucester MT Extra Condensed

Goudy Stout

Haettenschweiler

Harlow Solid Italic

Harrington

High Tower Text

Imprint MT Shadow

Informal Roman

Jokerman

Juice ITC

Kristen ITC

Kunstler Script

Lucida Bright

Lucida Calligraphy

Lucida Fax

Lucida Handwriting

Lucida Sans

Lucida Sans Typewriter

Magneto Bold

Maiandra GD

Matura MT Script Capitals

Mistral

Modern No. 20

Monotype Corsiva

MS Mincho

MS Outlook

MS Reference Sans Serif

MS Reference Specialty

MT Extra

Niagara Engraved

Niagara Solid

OCR A Extended

Old English Text MT

Onyx

Palace Script MT

Palatino Linotype

Papyrus

Parchment

Perpetua

Perpetua Titling MT

Playbill

Poor Richard

Pristina

Rage Italic

Ravie

Rockwell

Rockwell Condensed

Rockwell Extra Bold

Script MT Bold

Showcard Gothic

Snap ITC

Stencil

Tempus Sans ITC

Tw Cen MT

Tw Cen MT Condensed

Viner Hand ITC

Vivaldi Italic

Vladimir Script

Wide Latin

Wingdings 2

Wingdings 3

FONTS & TYPEFACES

Mac OS X +30

American Typewriter

Apple Chancery

Apple Symbols

Baskerville

Big Caslon

Brush Script Std

Chalkboard

Charcoal CY

Cochin

Cooper

Copperplate

Courier

Didot

Futura

Geneva

Gill Sans

Helvetica

Helvetica Neue

Herculanum

Hoefler Text

Lucida Grande

Marker Felt

Monaco

Optima

Papyrus

Tahoma

Taipei

Times

Zapf Dingbats

Zapfino

iLife '09 +13

Academy Engraved LET

Bank Gothic

BlairMdITC TT

Bodoni SvtyTwo ITC TT

Bradley Hand ITC TT

Cracked

Handwriting – Dakota

Palatino

PortagoITC TT

Santa Fe LET

Savoye LET

Snell Roundhand

Stone Sans ITC TT

iWork '09 +25 Fonts

Academy Engraved LET

Bank Gothic

Blackmoor LET

BlairMdITC TT

Bodoni Ornaments ITC TT

Bodoni SvtyTwo ITC TT

Bodoni SvtyTwo OS ITC TT

Bodoni SvtyTwo SC ITC TT

Bordeaux Roman Bold LET

Bradley Hand ITC TT

Capitals

Jazz LET

Mona Lisa Solid ITC TT

Palatino

Party LET

PortagoITC TT

Princetown LET

Santa Fe LET

Savoye LET

SchoolHouse Cursive B

SchoolHouse Printed A

Snell Roundhand

Stone Sans ITC TT

Synchro LET

MS Office for Mac 2008 +72 Fonts

Arial Narrow

Arial Rounded MT

Baskerville Old Face

Bauhaus 93

Bell MT

Bernard MT Condensed

Book Antiqua

Bookman Old Style

Bookshelf Symbol 7

Britannic Bold

Brush Script MT

Calibri

Calisto MT

Cambria

Cambria Math

Candara

Century

Century Gothic

Century Schoolbook

Colonna MT

Consolas

Constantia

Cooper Black

Copperplate Gothic Bold

Copperplate Gothic Light

Corbel

Curlz MT

Edwardian Script ITC

Engravers MT

Footlight MT Light

Franklin Gothic Book

Franklin Gothic Medium

Garamond

Gill Sans MT

Gill Sans Ultra Bold

Goudy Old Style

Gloucester MT Extra Condensed

Haettenschweiler

Harrington

Imprint MT Shadow

Lucida Bright

Lucida Calligraphy

Lucida Console

Lucida Fax

Lucida Handwriting

Lucida Sans

Lucida Sans Typewriter

Lucida Sans Unicode

Meiryo

Mistral

Modern No. 20

MS Gothic

MS Mincho

MS PGothic

MS PMincho

MS Reference Sans Serif

MS Reference Specialty

Onyx

Perpetua

Perpetua Titling MT

Playbill

Rockwell

Rockwell Extra Bold

Stencil

Tw Cen MT

Wide Latin

Wingdings 2

Wingdings 3

number of fonts
available on Windows

number of fonts
available on Macs

number of fonts available
on both Windows and Mac

Common Windows and Mac fonts

Out of the 131 possible Windows fonts and the 125 possible Mac fonts, there is a substantial overlap that we can exploit. This includes not only the core Web fonts but also the many fonts installed by Microsoft Office on both Windows and Mac versions.

Although the goal of fluid Web typography is to be prepared for the uncertain nature of displaying your designs in Web browsers, it's helpful to begin by identifying the cross-OS fonts. There are a total of 68 (59 Web safe plus the ten core Web fonts less dingbat fonts like Bookshelf Symbol 7, Webdings 2, and Webdings 3).

These 68 fonts make up the core of the list of Web safe fonts, giving Web designers a wide palette of text, display, and decorative fonts to choose from. While there is not a guarantee that all of these fonts will be present on the end user's machine, as there is with the core Web fonts, the likelihood is high.

Remember, though, that not every one of the 68 fonts is created equal, and not every font is readable at every size on the screen. Some of these fonts will be fine for body copy, but most are only suited for display copy (e.g., headers).

Cross-OS Web Safe Fonts

The 68 fonts likely to be available on both Mac and Windows computers above and beyond the ten core Web fonts. All fonts are displayed at 10px for relative size comparison.

Arial Narrow

Arial Rounded MT Bold

Baskerville Old Face

Bauhaus 93

Bell MT

Book Antiqua

Bookman Old Style

Bradley Hand ITC

Britannic Bold

Brush Script MT

Calibri

Calisto MT

Cambria

Candara

Century Gothic

Century Schoolbook

Colonna MT

Consolas

Constantia

Cooper Black

COPPERPLATE GOTHIC BOLD

COPPERPLATE GOTHIC LIGHT

Corbel

Curlz MT

Edwardian Script ITC

ENGRAVERS MT

Footlight MT Light

Franklin Gothic Book

Franklin Gothic Medium

Garamond

Gill Sans MT

Gill Sans Ultra Bold

Gloucester MT Extra Condensed

Goudy Old Style

Haettenschweiler

Harrington

Imprint MT Shadow

Lucida Bright

Lucida Calligraphy

Lucida Fax

Lucida Handwriting

Lucida Sans

Lucida Sans Typewriter

Lucida Sans Unicode

Mistral

Modern No. 20

MS Reference Sans Serif

Onyx

Palatino Linotype

Papyrus

Perpetua

PERPETUA TITLING MT

Playbill

Rockwell

Rockwell Extra Bold

STENCIL

Tahoma

Tw Cen MT

Wide Latin

OF EULAS, DRM, AND IP:
WEB FONTS AND THE LAW

Have you signed a EULA this month? This week? Today? In the past 5 minutes? You probably did and didn't even think about it or possibly even know that you had. A EULA (or End User License Agreement) is that long legal document you see before you run any application for the first time that you check off as having read (did you really read it?), that sets out everything that you can and cannot do with a particular piece of software, to protect the creators' rights to their intellectual property (IP).

Unlike an image, audio, video, or other media, a font is actually computer software that creates glyphs of a particular shape, and is therefore subject to EULAs as set by the type foundry or organization that is licensing or selling it. When you purchase a font—whether separately or as part of a package included with an operating system or application such as a word processor—you are granted certain rights to use that font. Although they generally include the right to embed the font in a digital document such as an image, PDF, or Flash movie, most EULAs do *not* include the right to embed the font in a Web page by downloading it using the `@font-face` rule. To complicate matters, there is no standard font EULA. They can vary greatly from maker to maker. If the EULA does not explicitly state that the font can be used for Web linking, then it is implicitly not legal to link to it for use in a Web page.

DRM and fonts

To protect digital files, creators often add digital rights management (DRM). Most common font files do not have the ability to include DRM, though, meaning that they can be downloaded and used legally or illegally as long as the browser recognizes the file type. Safari, Firefox, and Opera all recognize OpenType and TrueType fonts. Internet Explorer only recognizes the little-used Embedded OpenType (EOT) format, which Microsoft specifically created to add DRM to the font file, restricting its use outside of the browser and preventing cross-domain use. Fortunately, there are ways to convert TrueType and OpenType fonts to EOT and deliver font files specific to the browser's needs.

Keeping it legal

It is not the purpose of this book to encourage the illegal use of fonts. Type creators work extremely hard at their craft, and, like photographers, musicians, and filmmakers, deserve the fruits of their labor. However, while photography, music, and video have all evolved and flourished in the online environment due to their availability, typography has stagnated due to its unavailability.

I encourage everyone reading this book to purchase and use typefaces on the Web that have Web font linking as a part of their EULA, and to contact any foundry that does not explicitly state that its fonts can be used for Web linking. Unfortunately, it is incumbent on the font's user to look carefully through the language of the EULA for explicit permission to link fonts, and the language can be confusing. Some fonts are available for Web "embedding," which is different from Web linking. Web embedding covers use in Flash or text in an image, where the font file is not directly transferred to the browser, but embedded in another document (e.g., the image file or the Flash movie).

Even many "free" fonts do not include Web linking as a part of their EULA. In Appendix B, "Web Type Resources," you will find a list of font resources where Web linkable fonts can be downloaded.

Obviously, if you are using Web safe fonts—which the users already have on their machines—then there are no legal considerations for you. However, the safest rule of thumb when dealing with linking Web fonts is: *If in doubt, don't use the font.*

Font Embedding

Fontembedding.com

Although heavily biased toward EOT, Ascender Corporation's Font Embedding Web site has a lot of great resources for understanding the legal issues around Web fonts.

WEB FONT LINKING

Firefox 3.5, Safari 3.1, and Opera 10 support linking to TrueType and OpenType fonts. Safari and Opera also support SVG fonts, and Firefox 3.6 supports WOFF.

In theory, there is no reason why you should not be able to point a Web browser to a font file located on your Web server, have it download that font, and then use the font in your Web design—effectively linking the font file to the Web page. After all, this works just fine with images. Downloading fonts would seem to be the obvious solution for Web typography to be able to blossom, if only there were a way to tell the browser where the file is and how to use it. Surprisingly, there is a way, and it has been a part of the CSS standard for over ten years. So, where are all of the downloaded fonts?

The problems are deep and longstanding, centering around the concept of intellectual property (IP) and digital rights management (DRM). The impetus has been stronger to protect font files from illicit use than to use them in Web design (see the sidebar "Of EULAs, DRM, and IP: Web Fonts and the Law"). That is now changing, and there are a variety of new solutions:

⊙ **Linking**: All major browsers now support the linking of font files as described in this section. Firefox 3.5, Safari 3.1, and Opera 10 support TTF and OTF. Internet Explorer has supported EOT since version 4. Google Chrome .3 only supports linking with SVG fonts. Firefox 3.6 will also support the WOFF format.

⊙ **Services**: New Web font service bureaus provide easy font licensing and deployment. They come online as described in the next section.

⊙ **Technologies**: Techniques for embedding fonts with Flash and JavaScript have evolved.

Web font formats

In Chapter 1, I discussed the two most common font file formats—OpenType and TrueType. Although these are the font types that you will most likely find installed on your computer, it's important at this point, though, to consider all of the different file types that will allow you to display fonts in a Web page. Many of these are not truly new formats but are simply used to "package" an existing font file for use by Web browsers, generally adding some form of file protection and sub-setting.

OpenType (OTF) and TrueType (TTF)

OTF and TTF fonts are the most common file formats in use today. For more information, see "Modern digital font file formats" in Chapter 1. Currently, Firefox, Safari, and Opera all support OTF and TTF, with Internet Explorer being a notable holdout.

Embedded OpenType (EOT)

EOT fonts can be created by converting TTF fonts (and OTF if converted to TrueType first), encrypting them to prevent copying and to allow sub-setting to reduce the file size.

Developed by Microsoft in the late 1990s to allow Web font linking, the EOT format never caught on, despite being supported since Internet Explorer 4. This was because the format was not available for use in other browsers, so Web designers gave it a pass.

Although Microsoft finally submitted it in 2007 to be included as a part of CSS3, EOT was rejected and resubmitted to the W3C as a stand-alone standard in 2008, but it has now been superseded by the WOFF format (see below).

Internet Explorer supports linking to Embedded OpenType fonts.

Still in development, Google Chrome has already proved to be a popular browser. Although it is based on the same technology as Safari, it currently only allows font linking using SVG Fonts.

Scalable Vector Graphics (SVG)

OTF and TTF fonts can be converted to the SVG format to be transferred as vector data, and then used to render text in an HTML page. Fonts in SVG format can be sub-setted, and vector files tend to be smaller than other font file formats.

SVG is a Web standard set by the W3C for adding vector-based information to a Web page. Safari, Opera, Chrome, and Firefox all include native SVG support, while Internet Explorer still relies on a plug-in.

Since the SVG file can contain other data beyond the font rendering information, references to SVG files also include a reference to the anchored location (#) within the file of the font data:

```
fontfile.svg#FontInfoReference
```

Web Open Font Format (WOFF)

Like EOT, the WOFF format ecrypts OTF and TTF fonts, protecting them from being copied and compressing them for faster download.

A relative newcomer, WOFF evolved out of deliberation from the W3C's Fonts Working Group (discussed in Chapter 1). The format has already been rapidly adapted, with Firefox supporting it as of version 3.6, and several type services already offering this format as a part of their service.

Although new, this font format is widely regarded as the future of Web typography, providing ease of use and browser interoperability, while still ensuring IP protection for font vendors. However, this format will need to prove some value added over simply using raw OTF and TTF files, since these are more readily available.

Uploading fonts to a Web server

If you've ever uploaded a file to a Web server, then you know how to upload fonts. The process is virtually identical. Using your favorite FTP (File Transfer Protocol) application, add the font file to the directory of your choice, then use standard URL pathing to reference it.

Although you can place the file in any folder, I recommend creating a unique fonts folder to place all fonts in, similar to the way you might have CSS, JavaScript, or images folders for each of those file types.

If you are having trouble linking to fonts once they are uploaded, here are a few troubleshooting tricks:

◉ **Path**: Carefully check your path to be sure it is true match to where the file is located on-line. If you are using a relative path, try changing it to the absolute path.

◉ **Cross-domain**: Some font formats, font services, and browsers require that the location of the font be the same as the location of the HTML file requesting it, preventing the file from being called from other domains.

◉ **Server**: Check to make sure your server has the appropriate MIME types defined for fonts. MIME type identifies a particular type of file for the server by its extension (eg. HTML) and indicates the kind of data it will contain. A server will not be able to properly deliver the file to the end user. If you encounter a problem where your fonts don't seem to download, check with your systems administrator to make sure they have MIME types set up for .eot, ttf, otf, .svg, and .woff.

Determine file sizes to make sure that downloading fonts is a good use of bandwidth

Keep in mind that if you are using text in images, downloading a single font file may take less time. Also, fonts will be temporarily cached for use between pages in the same site, so that once it's downloaded, using the file on subsequent pages is almost instantaneous.

Although potentially much smaller than images with text in them, the size of the font files you are downloading still need to be considered as part of your overall page size. Font files vary in size, depending on several factors:

◉ **Number of glyphs**: The number of characters in the font's repertoire. Font sub-setting can radically reduce this number.

◉ **Font shape**: The complexity of the font's shape. More-complex shapes require more data to describe them.

◉ **Metadata**: The amount of hinting and kerning data. This information is used to ensure that fonts are legible in a wider variety of sizes and spacings.

◉ **Font format**: TTF, OTF, EOT, or WOFF. Simple fonts with basic Latin alphanumeric characters can be relatively small—25 to 50 KB—while more complex character font files can run into the hundreds or even thousands of kilobytes.

Combined File Sizes

Fontin Sans is made up of six different fonts for regular (29 KB), bold (29 KB), italic (29 KB), bold/italic (25 KB), and small caps (29 KB). If all five are linked to on a page, it will add up to a download of 141 KB.

Beyond the individual file's size, you may need to include different files for regular, bold, and italic/oblique, further increasing the amount of data to be downloaded. However, once downloaded, the files are cached and will be immediately available to other pages in the Web site, at least for that session.

Name ▲	Size
FontinSans	
5 items, 57.21 GB available	
📄 Fontin_Sans_B_45b.otf	29 KB
📄 Fontin_Sans_BI_45b.otf	25 KB
📄 Fontin_Sans_I_45b.otf	29 KB
📄 Fontin_Sans_R_45b.otf	29 KB
📄 Fontin_Sans_SC_45b.otf	29 KB

Linking fonts to a Web page

The syntax for requesting a font file from a Web server is straightforward, requiring you simply to supply the following:

- **Font-family name**: A name to use for the font in the document. You set what this name is, but you will need to keep it consistent throughout your code.

- **Source**: The URL to find the font file, either relative or absolute. This can refer to an EOT, WOFF, SVG, OTF, or TTF file, and a single `@font-face` rule can include multiple source declarations, allowing us to specify the best format for the browser being used.

- **Local name** (*optional*): Included with the source that defines the name of the font to see if it is already available on the end user's computer. If it is, then the browser uses the local version, without having to waste time downloading it.

- **Format hinting** (*optional*): The font file format—OpenType, TrueType, or SVG. Currently, Internet Explorer does not support this value and will fail to recognize any source value that includes it. We'll see later how we can make this work to our advantage.

- **Weight, style, or variant** (*optional*): Define the weight, style, or variant that the linked font is associated with.

Note that not all of the values are required in order to link to a font, and you can repeat the same attribute multiple times in order to tailor this rule for specific browsers, which we will look at in detail later.

A simple font link is included with your CSS styles, either in an external file or in the style tags:

```
@font-face {
  font-family: fontinsans;
  src: url('fonts/Fontin_Sans_R.otf' format('opentype'); }
```

This will load the OpenType font *Fontin_Sans_R_ 45b.otf*, located in a folder called *fonts*. The format value should be either OpenType or TrueType. You can now reference the font family in your font stacks as `fontinsans`.

```
h1 {
  font-family: fontinsans, helvetica, arial, sans-serif; }
```

Name your font family based on use

Notice in the previous example that I named the font family with a name that relates it to its filename. I could have called the font family just about anything—`header`, `font012`, `bob`, or `jabberwocky`. Currently, the common practice is to use the name of the typeface family being downloaded as the font family name. This makes a certain amount of sense, as it identifies which font is in use.

In practice, though, your typography can change for a variety of reasons during development and even after. As with CSS class or ID names, I recommend naming font families based on their function rather than what they look like. This allows you to change

§ Whenever you are using fall-back fonts in a font stack, it's important to consider using ones with similar kerning and widths so that they take up roughly the same amount of space, regardless of which ends up getting used. For more details, see "Creating Fluid Type Stacks" in Chapter 6.

the font used in your Web pages by simply altering the file source rather than having to perform a find and replace throughout your code. Here are some ideas for naming your font families:

- ◉ **Based on type role**: In Chapter 2, we discussed three primary roles for type—`text`, `display`, and `decorative`. I recommend these for naming your font families.

- ◉ **Based on copy placement**: You may want to use more recognizable terms like `header`, `body copy`, or `asides`.

- ◉ **Based on purpose**: If you will be using different fonts for similar purposes, number or add a letter identification such as `header01`, `header 02`, `header03`, etc.

- ◉ **Based on use in Web site**: If your typeface is specific to an organization or company, add that to the name. For example, my freelance company is called Bright Eye Media, so I might call a font family I use as part of my corporate ID `Bright Eye Media Header`, or just `BEM Header`.

Font Name Information

FontBook on the Mac will provide a wealth of information about any font you have installed, including its PostScript name, full name, and font family. Just choose the font and then choose Preview>Show Font Info (⌘-I). **Windows includes a similar utility in its Fonts Control Panel.**

Fontin Sans Bold

Fontin Sans Bold, 18 pt.

PostScript name	FontinSans-Bold
Full name	Fontin Sans Bold
Family	Fontin Sans
Style	Bold
Kind	OpenType PostScript
Language	Albanian, Basque, Cornish, Danish, Dutch, English, Estonian, Faroese, Finnish, French, Galician, German, Greek, Icelandic, Indonesian, Irish, Italian, Malay, Manx, Norwegian Bokmål, Norwegian Nynorsk, Oromo, Portuguese, Somali, Spanish, Swahili, Swedish
Version	1.000
Location	/Users/jason/Library/Fonts/Fontin_Sans_B_45b.otf
Unique name	JosBuivenga: Fontin Sans Bold: 2007
Manufacturer	Jos Buivenga
Copyright	Copyright (c) 2007 by Jos Buivenga. All rights reserved.
Trademark	Fontin Sans is a trademark of Jos Buivenga.
Description	Copyright (c) 2007 by Jos Buivenga. All rights reserved.
Enabled	Yes
Duplicate	No
Copy protected	No
Embeddable	Yes

The first release of Opera 10 has problems with font properties, only recognizing the last one declared.

Specify separate font files for weight, style, and variant, but only if needed

By default, linked fonts are not assigned a specific weight, style, or variant that they correspond to. Instead, the font, if left undefined is used whenever those styles are defined.

To define a particular font to be used for a particular combination of font attributes, you simply have to declare them within the `@font-face` rule:

```
@font-face {
  font-family: display;
  src: url('Fontin_Sans_B.otf' format('opentype');
  font-weight: bold;
  font-style: normal;
  font-variant: normal; }
```

Looking Glass

Fontin Sans

Looking Glass

Fontin Sans (bold)

Looking Glass

Fontin Sans (italic)

Looking Glass

Fontin Sans (bold/italic)

LOOKING GLASS

Fontin Sans (small caps)

In this example, the font *Fontin_Sans_B_45b.otf* will be used wherever the display font family is styled as bold, but not anywhere else. While obviously useful for adding different fonts for different CSS properties, it also means that each property will require a separate font file, and thus a separate download, adding to your Web page's download time.

Adding a local font name

If the users already have the font you want to down-load, then, like taking coal to Newcastle, you are wasting valuable time sending it to them. To ensure that a local version of the font will be used before a remote version is downloaded, add a local value, with the name of the font—either its PostScript name and/or its full name—with multiple values separated by commas:

```
@font-face {
  font-family: 'body copy';
  src: local('Fontin Sans Bold'),
       local(FontinSans-Bold),
       url('fonts/Fontin_Sans_B.otf' format('opentype');
  font-weight: bold; }
```

This tells the browser to see if there is a local version of the font available, first using the font name (**Fontin Sans Bold**) and the PostScript name (**FontinSans-Bold**) and, if so, to use that instead of downloading the file.

Be careful when testing your site with local values in place. If you have the font installed, which you probably do, then your browser will pull that version, meaning that if there is a problem with downloading the font, you may not see it.

One drawback to including local fonts is that Internet Explorer can't use them, and will ignore anything after it in the source declaration. How-ever, since we will need to deliver a different font file to work in Internet Explorer anyway, this can work to our advantage.

As with all font family names, if it is composed of multiple words, make sure the entire phrase is in quotes (double or single). For example, "body copy".

Adding Internet Explorer and Google Chrome support

So far, we've learned how to add OpenType and TrueType fonts to a Web page. Although Internet Explorer and Google Chrome cannot use Open-Type or TrueType font files, Internet Explorer can use EOT font files, and Chrome can use fonts created using SVG. Additionally, since Firefox supports WOFF, and it is likely to become the Web font file standard, we should go ahead and begin to support that format as well. All we have to do is create the fonts in those formats, and then add them to the `@font-face` rule.

There are several methods for converting fonts from OTF or TTF files to EOT, SVG, or WOFF. The easiest way, though, is to use an online service like Font Squirrel (*fontsquirrel.com*) that allows you to download a Web *font kit*, complete with OTF, TTF, EOT, SVG, and WOFF formats as well as all of the CSS code needed to implement. Unlike with the Web font linking service bureaus, you have control over the font files.

Font Squirrel gives you two choices for getting fonts. First, you can simply browse their extensive list of hundreds of free fonts that have already been converted to Web font kits and begin using them immediately. Simply click the link, and all of the font files are downloaded to your computer for you to upload to your server.

If you own your font files in OTF or TTF format and they are legal to be used for @font-face linking, Font Squirrel also provides a simple method for converting the files to EOT, SVG, and WOFF to cover all of your bases.

To use Font Squirrel @font-face Kit Generator

1   **Add one or more fonts to your kit.**

Go to the Font Squirrel @font-face generator page (***fontsquirrel.com/fontface/generator***) and click the Add Fonts button. You will be given the option of choosing one or more fonts from your computer, which will be temporarily uploaded to the Font Squirrel servers. The font(s) will appear in the list, showing the format, number of glyphs, and file size.

Microsoft offers the free WEFT tool to convert True-Type fonts to EOT format. However, the application has not been updated in almost ten years, is buggy, and is cumbersome to use. If you need to do it yourself, instructions for using the WEFT application are available on the book Web site at fluidwebtype.info/EOT.

2 Confirm that the EULA for this font allows Web font linking.

This is a good-faith effort by Font Squirrel to ensure that you honor the font's EULA. For more information, see "Of EULAs, DRM, and IP: Web Fonts and the Law," earlier in this chapter.

3 Set the font options:

» *Choose the font formats. I recommend choosing all formats, even the original, to keep all files together.*

» *Choose whether to "Subset Fonts," which allows you to specify which glyphs are included, reducing the file size. I highly recommend choosing this option.*

» *Choose whether to "Clean Up Outlines," which should be checked only if you see problems with the glyph shapes when they are displayed on your Web page.*

» *Choose whether to "Auto-Hint Glyphs," which replaces the font's own hinting instructions. Do not choose this option unless your fonts are crowded together when displayed on your Web page.*

» *If you choose to sub-set fonts (which you should have), now choose the glyphs to include in the subset. You will want to include all charterers that are likely to be used. I recommend including lowercase, uppercase, numbers, punctuation, currency, and alt punctuation.*

4 Download the font kit.

Click the Download Your Kit button, which will only appear after you choose a font and check the EULA confirmation. The kit, including the font in all formats you selected, is downloaded to your computer with sample HTML and CSS code.

5 Add @font-face code to your CSS.

In order to get all of the different font format types to place nicely together, we have to use a modified version of the `@font-face` rule. Because Internet Explorer ignores any source that includes local or format hinting, we can set a separate source for the EOT font. Set another source, including the local information, where to download the WOFF version, the SVG version, and then the OTF or TTF version. As with all CSS, the browser will try the first value first, trying each subsequent value until it finds one it can use.

You can make any changes desired to the code, and I recommend changing the family name to the form recommended above, and possibly changing the path, to place all fonts in a common folder in the fonts folder.

Font Squirrel uses code based on the "bulletproof" @font-face rule, conceived by Paul Irish (paulirish.com).

name you give the font

path to EOT file   local font names

```
@font-face {
  font-family: 'body copy';
  src: url('Fontin_Sans_R.eot');
  src: local('Fontin Sans Regular'), local('FontinSans-Regular'),
       url('Fontin_Sans_R.woff') format('woff'),
       url('Fontin_Sans_R.svg#FontinSans-Regular') format('svg'),
       url('Fontin_Sans_R.otf') format('opentype');
}
```

path to WOFF file   path to SVG file and anchor within file

path to OTF or TTF file

WEB FONT LINKING SERVICE BUREAUS

FONTS & TYPEFACES

The great advantage of any of these services, though, is that they have taken the grunt work out of identifying fonts with EULAs that will allow `@font-face` linking in Web pages.

One of the most exciting possibilities in Web typography is the Web font service bureaus that have started to appear. These services allow you to choose from a catalog of fonts you can easily purchase a license for, and provide code to add to your Web pages that takes care of linking the fonts for browsers that support @font-face linking (including Internet Explorer).

These services are still very young—some are still in development at the time of this writing—but they offer what might be the easiest and least controversial path forward for Web type. By controlling the font license and providing formats for the widest selection of browsers, they take a lot of the pain out of dealing with EULAs.

These services are not without their issues though:

◉ They currently have a limited (but growing) catalog of available fonts.

◉ There may be extra charges if you need to have the font locally to create graphic comps, or the font may not be available at all. Some fonts are free, but others are licensed separately for linking to Web pages and for local use.

Although not ready at the time of this publication, Fontdeck (fontdeck.com) is a Web font service bureau under development from Clearleft and OmniTI.

◉ The fonts will be delivered from third-party servers, so you are relying on their bandwidth for the speed of your site. While this practice is common for functionality like maps, analytics, and other functions on the fly, its success in delivering fonts on demand is still to be seen.

Typekit: Cafeteria-style font selection

Typekit is working with font foundries to develop font linking licenses that will allow you to shop for fonts to use with `@font-face`, but using JavaScript code to control access and protect the typefaces from illicit use without actual DRM. While its font catalog is currently only a little over 175, it is rapidly growing as more foundries agree to partner with them.

Typekit was clearly created with designers in mind. It enables you to control which fonts are applied to elements in a Web page directly in the Typekit. You don't have to touch the Web page's code at all, except initially to insert two JavaScript tags. Simple.

To use Typekit

1 Create a kit for each Web site.

After logging on to **typekit.com** (you will need to register first), choose "Add another kit" from the Active kit list.

> » *Enter a name for the kit and the domain (eg. **brighteyemedia.com**), and choose whether to include a colophon badge (a small image placed on the page that links to information on Typekit about the fonts being used), and click Continue.*

> » *Copy the embedded code provided and paste it into the Web pages of the domain you specified in the head. You can get this code again from Typekit, but you may also want to paste it into an easily accessible location, such as a notepad application. Click Continue.*

```
<script type="text/javascript"
    src="http://use.typekit.com/
    secretcode.js"></script>
<script type="text/
    javascript">try{Typekit.
    load();}catch(e){}</script>
```

» *Now, click "Go find some fonts."*

2 Add fonts to your kit.

Choose Add next to the font you want to add to the currently active kit (showing in the top right corner of the interface), or view to see more details about the font. You can also sort the fonts by style or tag, or by using the options on the right side of the screen.

3 Set selectors, weights, and styles for fonts.

Once you have added the desired fonts, click Launch Kit Editor in the top left corner. The Typekit Editor appears in a pop-up window displaying all of the fonts associated with a particular kit.

» *Choose any of the fonts and then specify the selectors (HTML, class, or ID) to use it with. You can also set these directly in your CSS, using the font name directly in your CSS with a -1 and -2 (for esample,* `'coquette-1'`, `'coquette-2'`*).*

Typekit says it splits fonts into multiple files to make it harder to copy the font and protect it from piracy.

» *Choose the weights and styles to be included. Remember that each of these represents a separate file download. Typekit displays the file size for each along with the total at the bottom of the window to help you optimize your download.*

» *Create a CSS stack with fallback fonts and the generic font family.*

» *This page also includes links to view the embedded code and to change the kit's settings, such as URL and name.*

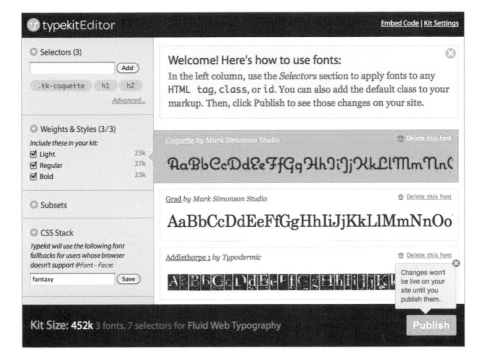

4 Publish the fonts to your Web site.

Click Publish. The changes will be reflected on your site in a few minutes. You can also add the two font names directly to your CSS font stack, overriding the code set in Typekit:

```
font-family: 'coquette-1', 'coquette-2', serif;
```

Kernest: An easy-to-implement solution

Kernest allows you to select from a rapidly growing catalog of over 500 fonts with a wide variety of license types, ranging from completely free to payment of a small fee per year per Web site.

Although Kernest's online interface still needs some development, it is easy enough to master once you get used to finding fonts. Adding fonts with Kernest's simple link tag makes it extremely easy to implement on any Web site and more reliable than solutions that use JavaScript.

To use Kernest

1 Find fonts for your Web site.

After logging on to *kernest.com* (you will need to register first), use the search field or scroll to the bottom of the page and choose Find More Fonts. It will be an option at the bottom of every page in the site.

» *From the list, choose a style, license type, foundry, designer, or family.*

» *All of the fonts for the option you selected will be displayed. It may take a moment for them all to "flip" from their fallback version to the actual font, as all of the font files are downloaded. You can choose to set the displayed font's size (defaults to 48px), and add the font to a comparison list.*

» *Click the font sample to view it in more detail. This page displays the different weights and styles available for the font, as well as the license price.*

» *To add the font to a new list, enter the URL for the intended Web site. If you already have added Web sites, you can check the sites you want to include the font in. Click "Add to Selected Websites."*

2   Add fonts to your Web site.

To view the fonts associated with a Web site and to grab the embed code you will need to add them, click Your Profile in the top right of the interface.

» *On the Profile page, all of the sites you currently have set up are listed with the link tag code you need to copy and insert into the head of your Web site's HTML code:*

```
<link href="http://www.kernest.com/
    www-speaking-in-styles-com.css"
    media="screen" rel="stylesheet"
    type="text/css" />
```

To edit a list of fonts for a site, click the site name.

» *On the list page, you can delete fonts by clicking the "Remove from Website" link below its name.*

3   Use fonts in your Web site.

The fonts you added using Kernest will now work just like any other Web embedded font using the `@font-face` rule. Simply add the name of the font to your font-family stack and watch the results. You can then add the font names to any font family declarations in your CSS (e.g., `font-family: 'BPreplay'`).

Typotheque: A font foundry goes it alone

Typotheque is a font foundry that is introducing its own downloadable Web font service that allows designers to purchase a single license to use its fonts both in print and on the Web. Although its catalog includes only a few dozen fonts, they are distinctive and high quality for both media.

The Typotheque interface is a little confusing at times but manageable. You can test fonts free for up to 30 days and see stats for their use on your site. Typotheque also includes an excellent font sub-setting system that can radically reduce the size of files being downloaded.

To use Typotheque

1 Choose and purchase fonts to use.

After logging on to **typotheque.com** (you will need to register first), you need to purchase a font license. Choose "fonts" from the left menu.

» *Choose the font you want to purchase from the list—don't worry, you can select the Trial Web License option and not have to pay anything yet.*

» *Click the Buy This Font button in the top right corner.*

» *Check which font option or options you want from the list and then the license type you want. Full License is for print and Web; Web License is much less expensive but only works for Web linking; or Trial Web license, which is free but expires after 30 days, when the font will no longer appear on your Web site.*

> » *When you are finished, scroll to the bottom of the page and click Continue.*

> » *Choose your payment option (if needed), check the box indicating that you have read the EULA, and then click Place Order. The font will now be available to you in your Web fonts.*

2 Create a project where the fonts will be used.

Click the My Web Fonts button or choose it from the main navigation menu under My Account.

> » *Choose either "Create a Project," or Edit, for an existing one.*

> » *Enter a name for the project.*

> » *Check the fonts you want to include. Each font family allows you to specify the font to be used for normal (N), bold (B), italic (I), and bold italic (BI).*

> » *Choose a language, whether you want to include small caps, and your numeral style (old style numerals look the best).*

> » *Enter a URL where the fonts will be used, and click the Save button.*

3 Insert the code into your Web site.

Back on the My Web Fonts page, click the Code button. Copy the link tag and paste it into the head of your HTML pages:

```
<link rel="stylesheet" href="http://
    test.typotheque.com/WF-secret-
    code#" type="text/css" />
```

My Web Fonts also has CSS code that you can copy and paste to add the different font families to your page.

WEB FONT EMBEDDING WITH JAVASCRIPT

As an alternative to using `@font-face`, there are ways to embed font data into Web pages that are cross-browser compatible using the JavaScript. While this allows you to use virtually any font (although EULAs should still be considered), using JavaScript for fonts is primarily intended for adding display fonts for headlines or other short blocks of text.

Font detection with JavaScript

lalit.org/lab/javascript-css-font-detect

Lalit Patel has created a JavaScript that "detects" whether a specific font is installed by measuring the width and height of the length of the text string mmmmmmmmmml at 24px. The script compares those values to the width and height of the default font. Since no two fonts will have the same values, the script uses these numbers as a unique fingerprint for the fonts.

lalit.lab

JavaScript/CSS Font Detector

on Saturday, March 10th, 2007 at 11:19 am

JavaScript code to detect available availability of a particular font in a browser using JavaScript and CSS.

I wrote a JavaScript code which can be used to guess if a particular font is present in a machine. This may be help of desktop-like web application developers when they want to provide different skins or fonts preferences to their users. This may also be help for blog skin designers which can provide different fonts for different users based on the list of fonts on their machine. Designers don't have to rely on the most common fonts like Arial, Verdana or Times New Roman. Since increasing number of users have modern PC with new operating system / applications, they may very well have a wide array of other common fonts in their machine.

How does it work?

This code works on the simple principle that each character appears differently in different fonts. So different fonts will take different width and height for the same string of characters of same font-size.

44 PX

Arial mmmmmmmmmml

Times New Roman mmmmmmmmmml

33 PX

Search

[_____] (Search)

Recent Posts

- Clever Google Ad Hack
- Vacation Relaxation?
- Looking for Geek Ninjas
- Nandan Nilekani, the proudest Indian in the world.
- Vanity

Tag Cloud

code office design prototype geeks environment quote synapse bhubaneswar

The most popular of these techniques is Cufón, which uses JavaScript to create and embed font data that is then used to render the text on the screen. The downside to Cufón is that all of the styles must be implemented through JavaScript, but that can also have its advantages over CSS. If you combine Cufón with JavaScript frameworks like jQuery, you can actually achieve text styles—like text gradients—that are currently impossible with CSS.

Additionally, since the fonts are reduced to JavaScript text files, they tend to be slightly smaller than the OpenType or TrueType files they are based on.

The Cufón solution is composed of a minimum of two JavaScript files: the rendering engine file (*cufon-yui.js*) and the font data file(s), which is named based on the font file name. Font families have to be processed through a font generator to be turned into JavaScript. You can have multiple fonts loaded for a single page, and font families are assigned to selectors using JavaScript rather than CSS, which can potentially interfere with styles set in CSS.

Cufón works only with UTF-8 encoded pages.

To use Cufón

1 **Download the Cufón code.**

   Start at *cufon.shoqolate.com*. Click the Download button to get the *cufon-yui.js* file, which you will need to upload to your server for easy access. This file is compressed for quicker loading.

2 Generate your JavaScript font files.

If you are not already on the Generator page, click the Generator button. This is where you will upload and enter all relevant information about your font.

» *Select the font files you want to convert, including a version for Regular and, optionally, versions for bold, italic, and bold/italic.*

» *Enter a name for this font and check the box indicating that the EULAs for those fonts allow for embedding. This is basically the honor system of DRM.*

» *Choose the glyphs to include in the font file. This allows you to subset the font and reduce file size. Choosing All includes every glyph in the font's repertoire but will lead to a large file size. I recommend using Basic Latin, which will include all of the most commonly used glyphs for Western languages. You can also specify particular characters by entering them into the field at the bottom of this area.*

» *Enter the domain or domains (separated by commas) in which the fonts are to be used. This prevents cross domain font sharing and may be required by the font's EULA.*

» *Set performance values. For the most accurate typeface rendering but slightly larger file sizes, check "No thanks, use the font's own value," uncheck "Allow path optimization," and keep "Include kerning tables" checked.*

» *If you are using Cufón with other scripts, change the function name call as needed; otherwise, move along, nothing to see here.*

> » *Check that you accept the terms of the MIT license that Cufón is using.*

> » *"Let's do this!"(click that at the bottom of the page). The JavaScript font file will be downloaded.*

3   Rename font files and make more.

The single file you created will contain all of the fonts you indicate in step 4. The filename will include the names of all of the font styles and the weights of the font expressed in the 100–900 scale, where 400 is normal weight and 600 is bold. I recommend renaming the file to just the font name and the weight and style abbreviated. For example, a font called

Fontin_Sans_400-Fontin_Sans_700-Fontin_Sans_italic_400-Fontin_Sans_italic_700.font.js

can be renamed simply to

Fontin_Sans-RBIBI.js

The "RBIBI" indicates that this font includes regular, bold, italic, and bold/italic versions. To create more font files, scroll to the top and repeat step 2.

4   Upload files to your server and link them to your Web page.

Once you have created all of the desired font files, upload *cufon-yui.js* and your font JavaScript files to your server.

> » *Add a script link in the head of your Web page.*

```
<script src="cufon-yui.js"
   type="text/javascript"></script>
<script src="Diavlo-RB.js"
   type="text/javascript"></script>
<script src="Fontin_Sans-RBIBI.js"
   type="text/javascript"></script>
```

» *Add default CSS to be used if Cufón is unable to load the fonts for some reason:*

```
<style>
  h1, h2 { font-family:
    impact, sans-serif; }
  p { font-family: 'franklin
    gothic book', serif; }
</style>
```

5   Use JavaScript to add font-family style.

To style your text, you will need to add your styles through JavaScript. Cufón has made this relatively simple by including a function that uses the selector and font family to apply the styles to the Web page:

```
<script type="text/javascript">
  Cufon.replace('h1', {
    fontFamily: 'Diavlo' });
  Cufon.replace('h2', {
    fontFamily: 'Diavlo' });
  Cufon.replace('p', { fontFamily:
    'Fontin Sans' });
</script>
```

Another alternative for adding specific fonts is using a Flash replacement technique called sIFR. Although I do not generally recommend using it, since it relies on the Flash plug-in, you can find instructions for using it at fluidwebtype. info/flash.

WHICH WEB FONT SOLUTION SHOULD I USE?

None of the systems currently available to embed Web fonts are a perfect solution, but all of them are rapidly evolving. Many of the problems that I point out with the technologies presented in this book may well be resolved in the near future. Additionally, new technologies are coming online all of the time. A few important features—such as not hindering SEO performance and selectable text—are a given for all of these technologies, although they are relatively new capabilities in Cufón.

Before making a decision on which solution to use for your Web site, check the current condition of each of the Web services or Web embedding technologies, and then consider the following:

⊙ **Browser support**: All of the technologies support the most recent Web browsers, although not all of them support older browsers. Fortunately, @font-face is supported by the majority of browsers currently in use. The Web font embedding technologies rely on Flash and JavaScript support, which, while seemingly ubiquitous, cannot always be assumed, especially in hand-held devices.

According to TheCounter. com, in June 2009, 7% of browsers either lacked JavaScript support or had turned it off.

⊙ **Available fonts**: The advantage of using @font-face or Web font embedding technologies is that you can use any TTF or OTF font available (although licensing should be considered). The Web font embedding services are limited to the fonts in their library.

◉ **Speed**: A primary consideration is how quickly the font will display on the screen. This is controlled by file size, server traffic, and rendering time. Consider these factors:

» *Web safe fonts are already on the end user's machine, so speed is instantaneous.*

» *Converting fonts to JavaScript may reduce file size, but will require more rendering time on the client side.*

» *As font linking services become increasingly popular, it will be important to make sure they can handle increased traffic without slowing down.*

◉ **License**: Each of the technologies has different licensing requirements for the fonts you want to use. The Web font embedding services provide licenses as a service, so no worries. The other methods, however, require you to have the correct license type to *legally* use the font.

tech	browser support	# typefaces/ file type	sub-setting	license required
Web Safe	FF1, Sa1, Op3, IE3, GC.3	68[1]	NA	NA
@font-face	FF3.5, Sa3.1, Op10	TTF or OTF	Yes[2]	Web linking
@font-face	IE4	EOT	Yes[2]	Web linking
@font-face	Sa3.1, Op10, GC.3	SVG	Yes[2]	Web linking
@font-face	FF3.6	WOFF	Yes[2]	Web linking
Typekit	IE4, FF3.5, Sa3.1, Op10	300+	Not yet	Provided
Kernest	IE4, FF3.5, Sa3.1, Op10	600+	No	Provided
Typotheque	IE4, FF3.5, Sa3.1, Op10	25+	Yes	Provided
Cufón	JavaScript enabled	TTF or OTF	Yes	Web linking

[1] Dependent on availability on end-user's machine. 131 fonts on Windows. 125 fonts on Mac. 68-font overlap.
[2] Only if processed through a service like Font Squirrel.

- **CSS compatibility**: @font-face and the Web font embedding services all work with CSS, but Web font embedding technologies require JavaScript to style the text. This can make it more difficult to style text, especially when using complex contextual styles or pseudo-classes.

- **Local use**: Can you use the font on your own computer to create graphic comps? If not, this might interfere with your workflow if you have to create very exact design specifications.

Web Font Samples

See how the same text can be affected by the different Web font techniques. The top left sample shows the text styled with defaults.

default

@font-face

Kernest

Typotheque

Typekit

Cufón

Type Inspirations

tap tap tap

Tasty iPhone apps served with advanced Web type.

taptaptap.com

Fronted by two-time Apple Design Award winner John Casasanta, tap tap tap makes some very cool iPhone applications. Their basic philosophy is, "Your tasks should be accomplished with just a few taps (hence the name 'tap tap tap')." Like the software they create, tap tap tap's Web site is simple and efficient, but the design can also be scaled up for their About page or blog.

How they do it:

Tap tap tap uses Web font linking to download an OpenType version of the font Fertigo Pro, created by Jos Buivenga and available for free from *exljbris.com*. Fertigo is then used throughout the site as a signature typeface for everything except the tap tap tap logo. Even though the site only uses a single typeface, by mixing a variety of weights, colors, and sizes, they ensure that the typography never gets boring.

We think that typography is black and white. It is the space between the blacks that really makes it. In a sense, it's like music—it's not the notes, it's the space you put between the notes that makes the music.

Massimo Vignelli
Helvetica

SCALE & RHYTHM

4

Spacing and alignment control how the text is comprehended through space and time. Learn to control the tempo of your message and guide the reader from beginning to end.

The carpenter's adage goes, "Measure twice, cut once." Giving careful consideration to the measurements and scale you are designing for is what separates good Web typography from great Web typography. Size and space add texture and flow to your text, improving the readability and clarity of what you are trying to say.

When typographers talk about "motion" in type, they are describing the way that a well-composed text will compel the reader's eye, moving it along from the beginning to the end with as little disruption as possible.

Pixel • The smallest element of information in an image rendered on a screen arranged in a two-dimensional grid as a series of dots or rectangles. Pixels are combined in red, green, and blue at various intensities to create thousands or millions of different colors.

Looking Glass

Helvetica Neue UltraLight

WEB MEASUREMENTS

Many designers want to define with exact precision the placement and size of elements in a Web design, similar to the way they might design for print or video. Those media are static—even video, which might move and be projected onto larger screens, but the aspect ratio does not change, so everything is scaled relatively. However, on the Web, you are dealing with a variable canvas, with its final size dependent on the whims of the reader.

Understand relative and absolute unit types

Keep in mind that although some units are traditionally associated with typography (such as points and picas) and others with measurements of distance (such as inches or centimeters), all units are available to set any size or dimension in a Web design. For example, you can set your font size in millimeters or the padding on a column in picas.

In Web design, sizes can be expressed in either absolute or relative terms. I'll explain later in this section which to use for a particular situation, but first review the different measurement types and the units at your disposal.

Absolute value units (*Table 4.1*) are used to precisely control sizes, so that they do not vary, regardless of the viewer's particular screen size, browser, or operating system. That said, even absolute units can vary between computers, generally because of operating system inconsistencies. This is the case with point sizes on the Mac versus on Windows.

Relative value units (*Table 4.2*) have no fixed size, but instead are calculated relative to another value, such as the parent element's size, or to the screen itself. Although less precise, relative values can be quickly scaled and changed without your having to recalculate all of their dependent values. For example, if you are using relative values to set the font size and line height, simply changing the font size will also change the line height proportionally.

Use points for print but never for screen

Although they're standard for print design, I'd discourage you from using point sizes when defining font sizes for the screen. The problem is the inconsistency between Mac and Windows monitor resolution settings.

By definition, a point is 1/72 of an inch, or 72 points per inch (ppi). On a Mac, the computer assumes a monitor resolution of 72 dots per inch (dpi), which also coincides with the number of points per inch. On the other hand, Windows computers assume your monitor displays 96 dpi. If the system is set for large fonts, then Windows compounds the problem, assuming 120 dpi. Unix systems can vary between 75 and 100 dpi. These

§ For more details on designing Web pages for print, consult Chapter 6, "Grid & Composition."

unit	name	description	example
pt	point	72pt = 1 inch	12pt
pc	pica	1pc = 12pt	1pc
mm	millimeter	1 mm = .24pc	4.17 mm
cm	centimeter	1 cm = 10 mm	.42 cm
in	inch	1 in = 2.54 cm	.17 in

Table 4.1
Absolute Value Units

unit	name	description	example
%	percent	relative to size of parent element	150%
em	em	1em = 100%	1.5em
ex	x-height	relative to height of lowercase "x" in the font	4.17 mm
px	pixels	relative to monitor's resolution	12px

Table 4.2
Relative Value Units

operating system assumptions result in the Mac OS rendering 18pt text at 18px text onscreen, the Windows OS rendering 18pt text at 24px onscreen, and Unix systems typically rendering 18pt text between 19px and 25px onscreen.

The upshot is that most Windows users see text that is 33% larger than text the same text viewed on a Macintosh if it was set using point sizes, rendering points all but useless for Web design onscreen. While most Mac browsers will try to adjust for this problem by increasing the base Mac font size to 16, some variance persists.

If you are designing a Web page for print (i.e., `media="print"`), however, then using point sizes is not only perfectly acceptable, but it is the preferred method for defining precise font sizes.

Use pixels for precision control, but know that you are taking control from the user

Pixel Mosaic

All images on the screen (fonts included) are composed of a mosaic of tiny dots called *pixels*.

Although it is possible to precisely control the positions of elements with any of the absolute units, pixels are the most natural way to define measurements for screen-based media. Despite having a "relative" size, pixels behave absolutely in relation to the screen resolution. Many modern Web designs are specified in pixels because it is the most universal measurement regardless of screen size, OS, or browser. Like atoms in matter, pixels are irreducible as the smallest unit of meaningful

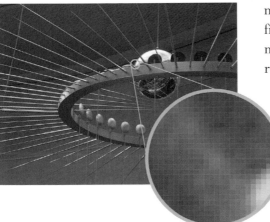

distance on the screen—you can't move something half a pixel.

While pixels give the designer precise control over where elements appear, they are not without their issues and inconsistencies. Most Web browsers allow users to enlarge text and zoom the page size, which is imperative for anyone with poor vision. Locking the font size with pixels or absolute values prevents Microsoft Internet Explorer from changing their size. Internet Explorer 7 goes some way in rectifying this limitation by allowing the entire page to be zoomed, but there is still some debate over pixels when accessibility is an issue.

Use ems and percentages for fluid design

In order to provide readers with the highest level of control over the content they are viewing, it is increasingly considered a best practice to define sizes (both font sizes and other length measurements) using relative units, especially ems.

The em (pronounced "m") is the fundamental unit of measurement in typography. It is defined as the size of the type as computed relative to the current size of the type of the parent element. For example, if you set the font size of your Web page to 12px, then .5em=6px; 1em=12px; 1.5em=18px; 2em=24px. If you change the font size to 14px, then .5 em=7px; 1em=14px; 1.5em=21px; 2em=28px. So, really, ems work like percentage values for sizing fonts. However, percentage and ems work differently for margins and padding, with percent-

For the sake of simplicity and clarity in the following examples, when expressing font sizes using ems, the assumption is that 1em = 16px unless otherwise stated.

12PX   **14PX**

.5em   .5em
6px   7px

1em   1em
12px   14px

1.5em   1.5em
16px   21px

2em   2em
24px   28px

§ Using ems and percentages, along with maximum and minimum heights and widths, is the only way to guarantee fluid designs and the easiest way to compose to scale, as explained later in Chapter 6.

Em Calculator

riddle.pl/emcalc/

There are a variety of tools that can help you calculate em sizes relative to a parent's pixel size. The best of these is Em Calculator, which color codes the different levels, making them easier to tell apart.

In this example, em sizes for different pixel equivalents are calculated to three levels.

ages being based on the parent's width or height and ems still being based on the parent font size.

One reason ems are not a popular solution is that, since their computed size is relative to their parent's size, you have to keep track of the current parent size to know how large or small the font will.

Despite their complexity, the advantage of using ems is that you can quickly change the scale of your design by simply changing a single font-size value. Since they are relative to the parent's font size, changing the parent's value changes the values for all of its children. Additionally, since some older browsers, most notably IE 6, will not resize text set in points, using ems guarantees that all of your readers get the same experience.

The bottom line is that whether you use pixels or ems is up to you. I recommend keeping them consistent within a document to avoid confusion.

🆔 **Em Calculator**		New version in the works	ver 2.2

SESSIONS SETTINGS	ABOUT	SPREAD THE WORD
New session [unsaved] (Save) (Delete)	Em Calculator is a small JavaScript tool which helps making scalable and accessible CSS design. It converts size in pixels to relative em units, which are based on a text size.	If you enjoy using Em Calculator, tell other people about it:

† Buggy on Opera & Safari (work in progress)

→ More

🦴 Digg It
📑 Bookmark on Del.icio.us
🗒 Bookmark on Ma.gnolia

Toggle

body { 16 px = 1.00em } ⌐

   node2 { 12 px = 0.75em } ⌐ ×

      node3 { 18 px = 1.50em } ⌐ ×

      node3 { 16 px = 1.33em } ⌐ ×

      node3 { 10 px = 0.83em } ⌐ ×

TYPE SIZE & LINE HEIGHT

In Web design, type size is set using one of two CSS properties, either `font`, which is a shortcut for setting several different font values or `font-size`, which is used only to set the size. The space between lines of text in a block can also be set in the font property or using the `line-height` property.

```
font: normal 16px/24px century, serif;
font-size: 16px;
line-height: 24px;
```

Setting Font Size & Line Height

Font sizes can be set as part of the font property short cut or independently.

Any of the relative or absolute size-value units listed earlier in this chapter can be applied to set the font size or line height. Or you can use specific keywords to set absolute sizes, which can then be adjusted with relative-size keywords. Line height can also be set as a numeric value, without any units, setting the spacing between lines as a multiple of the font size.

Understand how type is measured

A typeface's height is measured from the cap height (the height of the tallest capital letter) to the descender, with some breathing room added at the bottom to prevent characters on different lines from overrunning each other even if the line height is equal to the font size. The exact bottom buffer is set by the type designer. Taller uppercase letters— "b," "d," "f," "h," "i," "k," "l," and "t"— often rise slightly above the cap height but are not included in the measurement. Although each character in the font might have a different visual height, they occupy the same amount of space vertically, even if they do not fill it.

Even if set to the same size, though, a font's x-height will likely vary, leading some fonts to look taller than others, and often making them more readable, as is the case between Times and Georgia.

cap height

height

descender
buffer

The width of a character is simply its visual width plus any space beside it. The space may vary from letter to letter and can be *kerned*—the process of adjusting letterspacing to optimize the legibility of that particular font. The one exception to this is monospace fonts, which always occupy the same width regardless of the character.

Differing X-heights

The word "Fax" is displayed in Times and Georgia at the same font size, but notice that Georgia has a taller x-height. Taller x-heights can often make text more readable.

times   georgia

Size fonts with absolute keywords for consistency, and avoid relative keywords

In addition to specific units of measurement, you can set font sizes using relative and absolute keywords. The keywords are self-explanatory, as good keywords should be:

◉ **Absolute-size keywords**—*xx-small*, *x-small*, *small*, *medium*, *large*, *x-large*, and *xx-large*—set the type to a specific size as defined by the browser. Medium is the default browser font size.

◉ **Relative-size keywords**—*smaller* and *larger*—make text smaller or larger relative to its parent element's font size. Unfortunately, different browsers use different algorithms to determine the relative font size change, making them unreliable for browser interoperability.

In Quirks Mode, Internet Explorer 6 and earlier use "small" rather than "medium" as the browser default, and render the other keyword sizes correspondingly larger. As a consequence, authors using keywords should ensure that their documents are rendered in Standards Mode.

Table 4.3 presents the pixel equivalent size of each of the absolute-size keywords as well as the effect of the relative-size keywords. As mentioned, each browser has a slightly different algorithm for computing relative sizes, so there is some browser

Table 4.3
Font-size keywords with equivalent pixel sizes.

keyword	size (px)	smaller (px)				larger (px)			
		IE	FF	Sa	Op	IE	FF	Sa	Op
xx-small	9	6	8	9	8	10	10	11	11
x-small	10	7	9	9	9	13	13	12	12
small	13	10	10	11	10	16	16	16	16
medium	16	13	13	13	13	18	18	19	19
large	18	16	16	15	14	24	24	22	22
x-large	24	18	18	20	19	32	32	29	29
xx-large	32	24	24	27	26	48	48	38	38

DISPELLING THE ABOVE-THE-FOLD MYTH

For many years, the unbreakable rule of Web design was that if you wanted something to be seen, it had to be placed "above the fold." That is, it had to be in the space of the page that is displayed without scrolling in the Web browser. The term comes from printed newspapers. Important stories would always be placed at the top of the page, above where the paper was folded in half, since those were the stories people would see when the paper was in a vending machine or in a stack with other newspapers.

Applied to Web design, the theory goes that if you want to ensure that your readers see the text, image, or advertisement you really want them to see, it had better appear on the page first. This leads to using small text sizes; crowding columns of text, headlines, and advertisements as close together as possible; and generally cramming every last pixel available with content. This makes a certain amount of sense if your assumption is that viewers hate to scroll. You will then want to concentrate all of their attention on those first few hundred vertical pixels between the top and bottom of the browser window.

There's only one problem—this is a false assumption. At least it's an assumption that is no longer as true as it might have once been. Modern Web surfers do not fear scrolling, nor do they seem to pay any more attention to the content at the top of the screen than that down below. In fact, it's easy to make the argument that modern viewers have been trained to ignore the top of the screen because that's where all of the "junk" is, like navigation bars and advertisements.

The imaginary fold line has so many variables, including screen resolution, browser, operating system, not to mention the unknowable variable of how large the viewers like their browser window to open, that it becomes pointless to try to figure even an approximate value. Instead, your time is better spent creating engaging designs that are inviting and easy to scan.

For some solid research on the issue, consult ClickTale's Research Blog, December 23, 2006: Unfolding the Fold (*blog.clicktale.com/2006/12/23/ unfolding-the-fold*).

variance, which is compounded when relative sizes are nested. Microsoft Internet Explorer and Firefox are the most consistent, but even they vary when using smaller font sizes.

Although the range for absolute keywords is limited, they are an easy way to quickly apply a set scale to your type. Since relative font sizes are so inconsistently calculated between browsers, they are not recommended.

Setting type size to scale for fluid typography

Consider one fact of Web design: Everything on the screen is resizable, and there is *nothing* you can do about it. No matter what units you use, all it takes is a keystroke by the user to enlarge the text, potentially upsetting your carefully set type.

Learning to live with and take advantage of the vagaries of Web design will make you a better Web designer, and dealing with your font sizes expanding is no different.

So, the default size of text in a Web browser is medium or 16px. Rather than trying to set all of our font sizes individually, it is better to set a scale. Start with the body font size set to 100% (16px), and then use em values to scale from that size, as desired:

```css
body { font-size: 100%;
       line-height: 1.125em; }
h1 {   font-size: 2em; }
p {    font-size: 1em;
       line-height: 1.5em;  }
```

Setting a Fluid Font Size

This code sets the base font size to be whatever the default size is set for the browser (we can assume that it is 16px unless the user has adjusted the value), then enlarges that size for headers and holds the same size for paragraphs while increasing the line height.

If you then want to reduce the overall size of text on your page and you are using relative values, you need only change the percentage value set in the body. For example, 75% would create a document with a base font size of 12px, scaling all other sizes proportionally.

100% | 1em | 16px — **"What a curious feeling!"**

75% | .75em | 12px — **"What a curious feeling!"**

62.5% | .625em | 10px — **"What a curious feeling!"**

Alternatively, if you want more precise control, you can set a pixel value for the body font size to override the browser setting. This may cause some browsers to scale poorly, though, if the user manually increases the text size.

Size header and body copy to improve scannability and readability

Smashing Magazine has an excellent analysis of the use of font sizes and spacing in modern Web sites: **smashingmagazine.com/ typographic**.

One truism of the Web is that readers tend to scan a page. Once they find what they are looking for, they go into reading mode. While we will deal with a more holistic approach to creating scannable text in Chapter 6, the most immediate and reliable way to guide the reader's eye to important content is through a texture of type sizes. By treating the major page components—headers and body text—with a consistent scale for size, you can create a rhythm that improves scannability.

Heading sizes range between 18 and 32 pixels, while the most popular font sizes for body copy range between 12 and 16 pixels. Smaller font sizes for body copy may be encountered, but they are generally too small for comfortable reading and should be avoided.

A general rule of thumb is that the largest header font should be roughly twice the size of the body copy *or larger*,

```
body copy font size × 2 ≤ header font size
```

with the lower-level headers gradually decreasing, on a consistent scale, in size toward 1em.

Alice's Adventures in Wonderland

Alice opened the door and found that it led into a small passage, not much larger than a rat-hole: she knelt down and looked along the passage into the loveliest garden you ever saw.

h1=2em

p = 1em

One important factor to keep in mind while determining your font size is that 16px is the default font size set by browsers. Text is intended to be at least that large for easy reading. Many designers size body text x-small (10px to 11px) in the belief that it looks better and is easier to design with, especially if you are concerned with getting everything above the imaginary "page fold" or scroll line (see page 112 for more about this). However, larger fonts with a judicious use of white space will create text that is easier to scan and read. You need to give your body copy enough breathing room.

Choose a line height that gives your body copy breathing room

Beyond the size of the text, one of the most frequently overlooked factors in creating readable text is the line height and the width of the column in proportion to the font size. It's important to stress that line height is *not* the space between lines of text—as it is often mistakenly thought of—but the space from the baseline of one line of text to the baseline of the next line of text.

font size = 16px
line height = 24px

Alice opened the door and found that it led into a small passage.

A minimum font size to line height ratio of 2:3 is recommended for any extensive body copy:

$$\text{body font size} \times 1.5 \approx \text{line height}$$

So, a font size of 16px would require a line height of 24px or higher. To simplify matters, you could apply a line height of 1.5em, 150%, or just set a numerical value of 1.5. All of these will add the correct line height, regardless of how the copy is resized.

**Setting a Healthy
Line Height**

All four values will have the same effect on text with a font size of 16px.

```
line-height: 24px;
line-height: 1.5em;
line-height: 150%;
line-height: 1.5;
```

In addition to font size, column width affects the optimal line height. Narrow columns and shallower blocks of text, such as headers, require less line height to be quickly scannable. Generally speaking, you can reduce the font size to line height ratio in this case as low as 1:1.125. In order to preserve a more uniform page grid, however, designers often keep the line height consistent regardless of the column width, and use font, style, and color changes to better differentiate columns.

Easy-2-Read

informationarchitects.jp /100e2r/

Oliver Reichenstein's article in Information Architects Japan on making Web pages easier to read is not only exquisitely well laid out, but also extremely helpful for explaining why most people are using font sizes that are too small. He uses a simple optical test (with a photo provided by Michael Miner) to show that text in a magazine set at 11pt is much closer to Web text set at 16px.

Choose a column width that will not tire your readers out

Another important consideration for readability is the column width. Reading slows the longer a column grows—after a certain amount. A comfortable column width is easily derived from the page's base font size. Although not an absolute and dependent on the typeface, a good rule of thumb to determine a comfortable column width is to multiply the font size by 28:

```
body font size × 28 ≈ column width
```

This is a rough value. The multiple can range anywhere between 25 and 33, depending on your preference. Generally, though, if we assume a font size of 16px for our body copy, a comfortable column width will be around 450px.

Again, ems can come to our rescue to simplify matters, by allowing us to set a column based on the font size:

```
width: 28em;
```

Setting Column Width

Set a fluid width to take full advantage of the screen without creating uncomfortably wide text.

For a fluid design that makes optimal use of the available screen real estate, set the maximum and minimum column widths within the comfort range:

```
min-width: 25em;
max-width: 33em;
```

The column width will expand or contract as space is available within the Web design, but never stretch too wide or too narrow for comfortable reading.

TYPE SPACE

One way to add variety to your text is through the use of spacing between characters and words. Although not for everyday use, adding or subtracting space in your type is an important tool for creating fluid typography.

Letterspacing is **not** kerning, but it's all we've got

It's easy to confuse kerning with the practice of simply spacing characters farther apart or closer together. *Kerning* adjusts the spacing between characters in a proportional font; however, it will do this differently for different combinations of character pairs, allowing them to fit together optimally based on the font's own coordinate system. For example, the kerning applied to the letter pair "WA" is negative, so that the "A" slides in underneath the "W," increasing both letters' readability by reducing the optical space between them. The kerning for "UA", on the other hand, is 0, since there is no room to comfortably adjust the optical space.

In digital typesetting, kerning is automatically set by the font but can be adjusted. The base kerning between two characters is 0. You adjust the kerning with values between -100 and 200 (there are no units associated), which are applied to loosen (positive) or tighten (negative) the space between two or more letters in a block of text. Each letter is affected differently by the values, relative to the letters next to them.

In Web design, though, true kerning is not available. Instead, CSS offers the `letter-spacing` property to add tracking to text. *Tracking* is the ability to add a specific amount of space between

Kern: The Game

formationalliance.com

Practice your letterspacing skills in this Tetris-like game for the iPhone. Move characters to line them up in as tight a kerning as possible. The fewer points you are off in your kerning, the more points you score.

each character, regardless of the letters themselves. In theory, you could use this to adjust individual letters by placing span tags around one or more letters and then applying letterspacing:

```
.kern_neg2 { letter-spacing: -.2em; }
```

Using letterspacing to kern text:

The top version shows the word *wave* with no letter-spaced "kerning."

The second shows the letterspacing applied only to the letters "WA."

The third shows the same letterspacing applied across the entire word. Notice that the V and E are bumping into each other.

In practice, though, this technique is all but unworkable, since tags have to be placed for every instance where a kerning adjustment is needed:

```
<h1>
<span class="kern_neg2">WA</span>VE
</h1>
```

WAVE
WAVE
WAVE

Since different letters require different amounts of space added or removed to improve readability, and since so much content on the Web is dynamically created or contributed by writers who may not be able to control the code, this technique is only applied in extreme cases.

Use letterspacing or word spacing for effect, but use them sparingly

Both letterspacing and word spacing are blunt typographic instruments, coarsely adding space, regardless of the specific text. In general, the fonts you use in your design will already be carefully kerned by the type designer to maximize readability—if not, you probably need to pick a different font—so letterspacing and especially word spacing should not be necessary to improve readability.

There are times when you may want to add space in order to draw attention to text or to differentiate it from surrounding text, especially in titles and headers. Since this is done as a stylistic flourish rather than to improve readability, there are no hard and fast rules for how much space to add. It will be according to your design needs. To ensure that the text is easily scalable without having to adjust the spacing if the font size is increased, use ems, which will keep the same proportion at any font size.

ALICE'S ADVENTURES IN WONDERLAND

A L I C E ' S   A D V E N T U R E S   I N   W O N D E R L A N D

White Space Excitement!

Adding white space to give the title text breathing room activates even a simple title.

Set letterspacing for capitalized abbreviations and acronyms

One place where letterspacing is often needed is in abbreviations and acronyms. These strings of capital letters are generally spaced as if they were solitary letters, rather than as part of a group. If your HTML code is properly constructed, this should not be a problem, as long as acronyms and abbreviations use the abbreviation tag:

```
<abbr title="Cascading Style Sheets">
CSS</abbr>
```

CSS can then be used to style the abbreviation tag to tighten up the spacing by 5% or five-tenths of an em:

```
abbr { letter-spacing: -.05em; }
```

One potential issue is that not all abbreviations will need letterspacing. For example, the abbreviation for et cetera (*etc.*) is lowercase, and lowercase letters do not require tightening. So you only apply the abbreviation style to uppercase abbreviations.

You might also choose to set a negative letterspacing for long strings of numbers. This is a challenge, though, since there is no direct way to tag numbers in HTML without adding a span tag around the numerals.

CSS
CSS

Kern Strings of Capitals

The top example uses no letterspacing, and the bottom uses a very slight letterspacing to bring the abbreviation together.

HTML 4.1 also included the acronym tag, but it has been deprecated for HTML 5 in favor of the abbreviation tag.

Use indents or spaces between paragraphs, but not both

Traditionally, typographers separated paragraphs of text by indenting the first line of text by at least 1em with a space between paragraphs equal to the line height. The first line of the opening paragraph in a section would not be indented.

When the Web was first developed, though, there was no way to set a paragraph indent, and multiple spaces are always collapsed into a single space. To differentiate paragraphs, Web content producers began to simply add extra margin space between paragraphs, visually separating them.

Despite the fact that CSS long ago introduced the ability to add paragraph indents, separating paragraphs with additional white space has become the default standard style on the Web.

All paragraphs of text are automatically separated by the space of the line height. To calculate the optimal extra margin to add, multiply your line height by .75:

```
line height x 0.75 ≈ paragraph spacing
```

So, if your line height is 24px, then the optimal margin would be 18px. In theory, you should add this to either the top or bottom margin of the paragraph. However, one feature of modern Web browsers is that they will *collapse* top and bottom margins between elements, using the larger value as the only margin between the elements, ignoring the smaller value.

'Well, I should like to be a LITTLE larger, sir, if you wouldn't mind,' said Alice: 'three inches is such a wretched height to be.'

'It is a very good height indeed!' said the Caterpillar angrily, rearing itself upright as it spoke (it was exactly three inches high).

'But I'm not used to it!' pleaded poor Alice in a piteous tone. And she thought of herself, 'I wish the creatures wouldn't be so easily offended!'

'Well, I should like to be a LITTLE larger, sir, if you wouldn't mind,' said Alice: 'three inches is such a wretched height to be.'
    'It is a very good height indeed!' said the Caterpillar angrily, rearing itself upright as it spoke (it was exactly three inches high).
    'But I'm not used to it!' pleaded poor Alice in a piteous tone. And she thought of herself, 'I wish the creatures wouldn't be so easily offended!'

Indicating a New Paragraph

The top example shows paragraphs spaced apart, while the lower example shows paragraphs indicated by an indent, except for the first paragraph.

Known as *margin collapsing*, this means that you not only can, but should set the margin for the top and bottom of paragraphs to the same value:

Add Equal Margin to Top and Bottom

Since margins collapse to the largest value, add space above and below the paragraph.

```
p { font-size: 16px;
    line-height: 24px;
    margin-top: 18px;
    margin-bottom: 18px; }
```

This also ensures that the first and last paragraphs in your body copy can have top and bottom margins. The above code renders a total space between paragraphs of 42px as measured from baseline to baseline.

If you want to use indents, then you will need to remove the margin between paragraphs and add the desired indent, generally equal to twice the current font size or larger. If this is the first paragraph in a section, you will not want an indent:

If Indenting, Don't Indent the First Paragraph

Set top/bottom margins to 0 and make sure that the firs paragraph in a series is not indented.

```
p { font-size: 16px;
    line-height: 24px;
    margin-top: 0;
    margin-bottom: 0;
    text-indent: 32px;}
p:first-child { text-indent: 0; }
```

This will help with the scannability of the text, especially if you use a separate style for the first character and/or first line of text at the start of a section.

TEXT ALIGNMENT

Text alignment is generally taken for granted on the Web—left alignment suits most purposes most of the time. In order to create a sense of rhythm and movement on your page, helping to guide the reader's eye around and adding visual interest to the page, a little alignment variation can go a long way.

Set body text alignment to minimize gaps and maximize scanning

Text alignment in Web pages is, by default, to the left, with ragged edges on the right. Justified text—sometimes called *newspaper columns*, where both edges of the text are aligned—is rare on the Web.

```
text-align: left;
text-align: justify;
```

In print, justified text is created using a variety of techniques including word spacing, letterspacing, hyphenation, and glyph reshaping. In addition, well-formed justification is calculated on a paragraph level to prevent "rivers" of white space flowing down the middle. On the Web, unfortunately, justification is simply created by adding small amounts of space between words. On the screen, where you can only add whole pixels, this often results in uncomfortably large amounts of space between some words, especially in narrower columns.

Hyphenation is inexplicably absent from CSS. While it is proposed for inclusion in CSS 3, no work has currently been done on it.

When choosing to use left or justified alignment, keep in mind these factors:

⊙ Justified text is often seen as more formal and structured, while left alignment is more informal and approachable.

⊙ Justified text reinforces the grid structure of a page but can be harder to scan, since it often creates rivers of white space throughout the text, which interrupts the eye path.

⊙ Left-aligned text adds an element of white space to the right edge, softening the overall appearance of the page.

Combining Alignments

craigmod.com

Craig Mod combines right- and left-justified columns of text to create motion and rhythm around his page.

Center or right-justify text for effect and variety

More rarely used, centering or right-justifying text can create a specific feeling on the page.

```
text-align: center;
text-align: right;
```

Centering and right aligning text is integrally dependent on the design you are creating and how you want your readers to scan the page. While using a variety of justifications helps create rhythm and motion on your page, it can quickly seem cluttered or obnoxious. Always have a specific purpose for the variance of alignment, and use it sparingly. Here are a few ideas:

◉ Bulleted or numbered lists should not be centered or right aligned, as this makes them harder to scan by moving the beginning of each line around.

◉ Center section or module titles/headers if you want to make your site look a little different. Generally, section titles are best when left aligned, but centering them gives your designs a unique feel and may also improve scannability.

◉ Right-align text in the left column of a page or table if it helps show a closer relationship between the elements in adjacent columns.

Centered Section Titles

jontangerine.com

Jon Tangerine combines centered subheadings with justified text in his blog (detail shown) to create solid structure with visual movement.

Web Fonts: Then & Now

WEB FONTS have been with us for a decade. They were an original part of the CSS2 recommendation in 1998. Recently, the godfather of CSS, HAKON WIUM LIE, brought them sharply into focus with articles in CNET and A LIST APART. The ironic thing is, IE has supported web fonts using the EMBEDDED OPEN TYPE (EOT) format since 1997. The problem *was* that EOT was a proprietary format, belonging to Microsoft. Not for much longer: it's BEEN SUBMITTED TO THE W3C and is going through the process towards becoming a web standard.

§ In this chapter, we are only considering spacing issues with blockquotes and citations. Chapters 5 and 6 offer other ways to style text, including weights, italics, backgrounds, and borders. These can be deployed to creatively display longer quotations.

Blockquote Ideas

css-tricks.com/examples/ Blockquotes

CSS-Tricks has a page of blockquote ideas with sample code.

Increase margins for longer quotations and style the citation

Short quotes of less than three lines are included in a paragraph surround by quotation marks, requiring no other special formatting. In HTML, the blockquote tag is used to set off a block of text as a quotation, generally of two lines of text or longer. The quotation should be styled to distinguish it from other text by indenting its left and right margins and increasing the top and bottom margins. The amount of left/right indentation is based on the width of the column and then adjusted so that it does not conflict with any other indents. A good measure to offset blockquotes is to double the font size (2em), although more or less space may be required for wider or narrower columns:

```
blockquote { margin: 2em; }
```

This will clearly space the blockquote away from the rest of the text, but it's also up to the copywriter to make it clear that the text is a quote and to supply its source, possibly using the `cite` tag, which indicates a citation. Turning the `cite` tag into a block-level element and right-aligning it when it is included in a blockquote creates a strong style.

```
blockquote cite {
    display: block;
    text-align: right; }
```

The code above will force any text marked by the citation tag to a new line and right-align it.

Set footnotes and scientific or mathematical annotations using positioning rather than vertical alignment

Vertical text alignment allows you to adjust the position of inline text in relation to its natural baseline, shifting it up or down. For footnotes, mathematics, and scientific notation, it will not be enough to simply raise or lower the characters; you will also need to reduce their size relative to the surrounding text. These styles can be applied to the superscript and subscript tags, setting the vertical position to the baseline and then setting a position relative to that:

```css
sup, sub {font-size: .5em;
          vertical-align: baseline;
          position: relative;   }
sup { top: -.65em;   }
sup.math { top: -.8em}
sub { top: .2em; }
```

Although vertical-align provides several values to set the vertical position of the text, these have proved to be unreliable in multi-column layouts. The exact values will vary depending on the font, and you may also need to add some left/right margins to add breathing room.

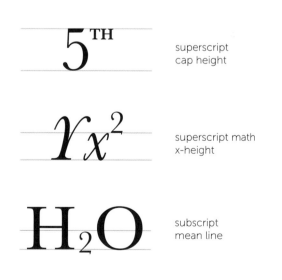

superscript
cap height

superscript math
x-height

subscript
mean line

Type Inspirations

Jon Tangerine

Beautiful typographic contrast.
Insightful typography editorials.

jontangerine.com

Jon is a designer living in Bristol, UK, with some of the cleanest pure Web typography I've seen. On top of this, his information and opinions on Web typography are required reading for anyone interested in the ongoing issues we face.

How he does it:

Jon uses a font stack of Web safe fonts, including Cochin, Baskerville, and Palatino Linotype, down to Georgia. He then combines a wide variety of sizes, styles, weights, and colors all scaled and spaced within a strong grid to provide clear eye paths and legible text.

We are told that typography has tended to evolve toward transparency, the optimal interface being viewed as one which the reader is least conscious of... To accept this too literally is to rule out designs which allow our awareness of the interface to constitute a major and ongoing aspect of textual pleasure.

William Gibson
Ray Gun: Out of Control

EMPHASIS & CONTRAST

Styles determine the impact your text will have on the reader. Use styles judiciously to add highlights and counterpoints to your message without bludgeoning the reader.

GUIDING THE READER'S EYE

The purpose of type is to portray the glyphs of a written language for reading by human beings. Beyond creating readable text that communicates your message, one of the other chief goals of great typography is to help guide the readers' eye around the page, helping them scan and find the content they are looking for.

Font Family • The collection of all fonts with the same name, but different weights, styles, variants, and stretch. The base font of the family is referred to as the *Roman* version.

Scannability is an important factor in all Web typography, almost as important as readability. Research shows that people read differently onscreen than they do in print, tending to want to access shorter chunks of content at a glance.

Looking Glass

TRASHED

looking Glass

Acid Reflux

Typography as a design element

In the 1970s and 80s', the photocopy machine came into its own as a way of quickly reproducing content on a large scale. Although they had been around for decades, it was during this period that the price became low enough that access was not only easy but common. Up until then, typography had been the domain of "professionals" who took their craft seriously (possibly a little too seriously). The ubiquity of the photocopier led to a lot of experimentation. Type was often used not just to communicate a written message but also as a part of the design itself, sometimes divorced from specific textual meaning'.

Of course, the use of text for ornamentation was nothing new, but with the advent of mass reproduction came a whole new style: The "grunge" design movement of the 1990s was

Ray Gun Magazine

The now-defunct magazine *Ray Gun* was renowned for its experimental typographic styling, which helped spearhead the grunge design movement of the early 1990s.

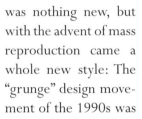

best exemplified in the rock news magazine *Ray Gun* and had a strong impact on early Web design, coinciding with and influencing the burgeoning field of Web design especially in the United States.

There is a lot of debate about using typography for decoration, and not just for clearly informational purposes. Some say that using type decoratively adds design texture, while others argue that it just adds noise. It will be up to you to decide how much (if any) text ornamentation will add emphasis and contrast to your designs. Don't be afraid to experiment.

Readability vs. legibility vs. scannability

Legibility, readability, and scannability are often thought of as synonyms, but in Web typography, it is important to separate them.

- ◉ **Legibility**: Type that is well designed and easily discerned. This is the responsibility of the type designer.

- ◉ **Readability**: Text that is easy on the eyes for the purposes of reading, especially over large blocks of text. This is the responsibility of the typographer.

- ◉ **Scannability**: Text that can be quickly surveyed for information relevant to the reader. This is also the responsibility of the typographer.

All three are important for successful content, but it is the last two that are where we apply typography, especially font weights, italics and obliques, decorations, text case, and color. Typography can either guide the reader's eyes around the page or obstruct their path.

Eye Tracking

Web designers often study how a reader's eye moves across the page in response to visual stimuli, with places where the eye rests being of particular interest. Such eye-tracking studies help us better understand how to help guide the user to important information.

WEIGHT

Font Weights

The nine font weights and their equivalent font names, shown using Museo Sans. Gray indicates that a font for that weight was not available, so the next closest weight is used.

If you are familiar with typography only on a word processor, then the concept of making text bold will seem straightforward—text is either darker (bold) or it is not (regular). However, typefaces often include a wide variety of weights ranging from thin to heavy.

There is more than just one bold, but not all of them are always available

For the most part, font weights are specified as either *bold* (darker) or *normal* (regular). Open type fonts, however, can specify numeric weights ranging from *100* to *900* in increments of 100 (i.e., there is a font weight 300, but not a font weight 367). Each of these weights corresponds to a specific weight name or names used by the font. For example, if the font's name is Myriad Pro Light, then it corresponds to a weight of 300. Additionally, fonts can be weighted relative to their parent element's font weight, either *lighter* or *heavier*.

```
font-weight: bold;
font-weight: 200;
font-weight: lighter;
```

Unfortunately, there are some browser inconsistencies with using numeric and relative values. The CSS standard states that if a numeric value is applied for which there is no font (i.e., the weight is not available for the typeface or its correspondingly named weight), then the browser should use the closest available weight. This is what browsers do, although they can sometimes disagree on exactly which value is the "closest." There are also discrepancies between how *lighter* and *bolder* act on a font weight, especially between Microsoft Internet Explorer and the other popular browsers. *Table 5.1* shows how CSS defines the effect of relative weights and how the relative values are treated in the most recent versions of the popular browsers.

Another obvious problem with using more than the basic bold weight is that if the font does not have the specified weight, the browser is likely to use the standard bold version, synthesize the weight (see "Browser-Synthesized Fonts," later in this chapter), or use no weight change at all. Coupled with the fact that none of the core Web fonts or cross-OS Web safe fonts have anything other than the basic bold, multiple weights are currently rarely used. However, now that downloadable fonts are more common, designers will be able to make use of a wider variety of font weights.

Safari 3 and earlier only rendered type weights at 400 (normal) and 700 (bold). Lighter always made the font weight normal, and bolder always made the font weight bold.

Table 5.1 Font Weights

The effects of the relative font weight values lighter and bolder vary slightly from browser to browser but most especially from the CSS standard.

parent weight	lighter					bolder				
	CSS	IE	FF	Sa	Op	CSS	IE	FF	Sa	Op
100	100	100	100	100	100	400	400	200	200	200
200	100	100	100	100	100	400	500	300	300	300
300	100	200	200	200	200	400	600*	400	400	400
400	100	300	300	300	300	700	600	500	500	500
500	100	300	400	400	400	700	800	600	600	600
600	400	300	500	500	500	700	900	700	700	700
700	400	400	600	600	600	900	900	800	800	800
800	400	500	700	700	700	900	900	900	900	900
900	400	600	800	800	800	900	900	900	900	900

* Weight always synthesized by browser.

BROWSER-SYNTHESIZED FONTS

When a font weight, style, or small-cap is specified in a design through the CSS for a particular font family that does not have that specific face, the browser will create that weight and/or style from its roman (normal). Synthesizing a font takes place within the browser on the fly, using data about units per em, bounding box coordinates, and specific Unicode character widths:

- ◎ **Bold**: Expands the outline of the roman proportionally to make it thicker.

- ◎ **Italic/oblique**: Slants the roman font to the right approximately 10°, creating a synthesized oblique.

- ◎ **Small-caps**: Reduces the height of capitals used for lowercase to the x-height of the font.

There are several problems with browser-synthesized fonts, most notably that they are created on the fly with no human interaction. Therefore, they tend to be less legible than a true version of the font, which includes appropriate spacing data specific to the font's needs. Beyond that, each browser will synthesize the fonts slightly differently, so synthesized bold fonts in Firefox may not look the same as synthesized bold fonts in Internet Explorer.

roman

Glass

true italic

synthesized oblique

Avoid using a typeface that does not have a true version of the particular style you need. If the browser synthesizes the font, it generally does so with no understanding of the typeface, often leading to a poor result. The reader may not be able to pinpoint why the font looks odd, they will just know that it doesn't look right.

Make text strong for impact, but don't beat your reader to death with it

Bold type is overused in Web design. In addition to the `bold` and **strong** HTML tags, all of the header tags (`h1`–`h6`) have a browser default style of bold. Even just relying on the browser defaults can lead to a lot of dark text on the screen. Since darker text is perceived by the human eye as important, the overuse of bold text can lead to the viewer's eye darting around the page with nowhere to rest. If everything is important, then nothing is important.

Although most commonly associated with the `bold` tag, bold style is also applied to the **strong** tag. Since not all languages make text bold to indicate importance, use the **strong** tag.

Here are a few suggestions that will help keep your typography subtler when using bold fonts:

◉ **Do not rely on the default styles.** Begin by setting every tag's font weight to normal, as explained in Chapter 6, "Grid & Composition." From there, add bold judiciously to a select number of elements that you truly want to attract your reader's attention.

◉ **Combine bold with size and color changes to soften the effect of the bold.** For example, make the text bold, but use a lighter color on a light background to soften the contrast.

◉ **De-emphasize to emphasize**. A reader's eye seeks areas of difference in a design. So, if everything in a design screams for readers' attention, it's the area of "calm" that they will look at. Sometimes it's best to lighten rather than bold text in order to draw attention to it.

Combining Styles, Weights, and colors

seedmagazine.com

The Web site for *Seed* magazine combines many different techniques, including weight, text case, color coding, and contrast, to guide the reader's eye around the front page.

ITALIC & OBLIQUE

In CSS, *font style* refers to whether a typeface uses an *italic* or *oblique* version. These are often used to indicate that text is a citation to another work or simply to add emphasis. In typography, *normal* text refers to the *roman face* (also called *regular*), in contrast to the italic face. Oblique type is referred to as *sloped roman*.

Oblique is not italic, but they are often used synonymously

Italic fonts were originally developed as the more script- or cursive-looking alternatives within a typeface family. They were created as unique glyphs, stylistically similar but distinct from the roman version. Italic fonts have the added benefit of being slanted, usually taking up less horizontal space, and therefore allowing for tighter printing.

Glass

roman (regular)

Glass

italic

```
font-style: italic;
```

Oblique type is often confused with italic, because they are both set at an angle and are used interchangeably in typography. However, unlike italics, an oblique is not a unique glyph. It is simply the roman face slanted at an angle of anywhere from 2° up to 20°—but generally around 10°—and then adjusted by the type designer for optimal legibility.

Glass

roman (regular)

Oblique

```
font-style: oblique;
```

While it's not an absolute rule, serifed type-faces often include an italic version, while sans-serif fonts use oblique. This is true of some sans-serif typefaces even if the font is called italic. The "italic" is actually a slanted version of the roman with no unique glyphs.

In theory, when you refer to an oblique font in your CSS, you should get slanted roman type, regardless of what fonts are available in the type-face. In practice, however, browsers always use the italic version of a font if it is available, regardless of whether you specify italic or oblique for the font style. If neither an oblique nor an italic version of the typeface is available, then the browser will synthesize one, which is generally undesirable for quality typography.

Add emphasis to highlight important concepts and ideas

In addition to the `italic` HTML tag, the `cite` and `em` (emphasis) tags default to an oblique or italic font style for their text. As with bold text, italic/oblique fonts should be used sparingly, and only with a specific purpose, since they are intended to differentiate content. For example, some books (such as this one) set an introductory blurb to a chapter in italics or oblique in order to highlight it as the starting place. Here are few ideas for italicizing or obliquing text:

- **Book titles**, which is why this is the default style for the citation tag, should be used to style book titles.

- **Important terms** appearing for the first time.

- **Block quotes** or other aside text.

- **Hypertext links**, used as an alternative method for underlining links.

DECORATION

Just say no to the `blink` property. Not only is it the most annoying style ever conceived, it's also being deprecated as of CSS Level 3.

Promotions
<u>Get Hotel+Air+Car</u>
<u>Meetings</u>
<u>Book Now & Save</u>

Promotions
Get Hotel+Air+Car
Meetings
Book Now & Save

Unlike other typographic styles, text decoration styles do not change the individual characters, but are applied equally across a block of text. While there are currently only a few limited text decorations, and I recommend avoiding most of them, new decorations are on the way in CSS3.

Do **not** use `underline` to underline links

While it is the default style given to links, and it is true that users respond to underlined text as hypertext links, the `underline` style is a crude and unattractive way to underline link text. `Underline` places a rule (line) 1px below the baseline of the text in the same color as the link, adding visual noise to the design and obscuring any character's descenders.

Additionally, not all links are created equal. Simply underlining a large list of links does little more than add clutter, interfering with scannability. Although adding white space can improve this, there is a better way to underline links, which I'll explain later in this chapter (in "Color"). Turn underlining off for all links, and then add the underlining back selectively, depending on context.

```
a { text-decoration: none; }
```

One other place that `underline` is used is with book titles, but that's a holdover from typewriters, and book titles should now be italicized, really leaving `underline` with nothing to do.

Use strike through to indicate deleted text

One case where text decoration can be useful is indicating that a particular block of text has been deleted or edited. Use the `line-through` property, which places a rule through the mean line of each character affected. The best way to accomplish this is by creating a specific class that can be applied to HTML text using a span tag:

Trash, trash, yes, yes. Come with us into the wonderful world of trash the Cape Arcona Type Foundry offers you ~~The Cape Arcona Trash Pack~~ Arconas finest grunge fonts: CA BND Trash™, CA Coronado™, CA Mosk Trasher™ and CA Wolkenfluff™ for an incredible price of just €49 (regu ~~Trash Pack is available until 21. August 2009, so buy the package befe~~ it's not available anymore.

```
.deletetext {
    text-decoration: line-through; }
```

Deleted Text

In the above example, the offer date has passed, but rather than removing the information, the date is struck out and a new message (in bold) is placed after.

Text shadows add depth, but do not rely on them to convey information

Although not officially a part of the CSS specification yet, text shadow will be in the forthcoming CSS Level 3 spec, and Safari, Firefox, and Opera have all implemented the style. Add a shadow underneath any text, controlling the left/right and up/down offset, as well as the color:

```
text-shadow: -2px 2px 10px rgb(0,0,0);
```

Since Microsoft Internet Explorer has not implemented text shadow, you should never rely on it to convey critical information, such as link text, but it can make a nice addition with rollover to link text.

You can combine the text shadow with a transparent color to control the darkness of the shadow and include multiple text shadows just by repeating the values separated by a comma:

```
text-shadow:
    0 0 10px rgba(0,255,0,.5),
    -10px 5px 4px rgba(0,0,255,.45),
    15px -4px 3px rgba(255,0,0,.75);
```

Although text opacity is better set using the RGBA format, explained later in this chapter, `opacity` and the Internet Explorer equivalent, `filter:alpha()`, are more universally available.

When you set the text to be slightly transparent, the background color tints the glyphs, creating a harmonious tone. This can be used to highlight certain text—for example, emphasized or link text. Then you can change the opacity when the text is hovered over with the user's mouse:

Opacity

The text is shown at an opacity of 1 (top), .75, .5, and .25.

```
em { opacity: .75;
        filter: alpha(75); }
em:hover  { opacity: 100;
        filter: alpha(100); }
```

TEXT CASE

Text should already be set in the correct case by the system, but there will be times when you are not sure what case the text will be—for example, if it is being dynamically provided by a database— or when you might want to change the case for emphasis, such as in header text.

text case

lowercase

Text Case

capitalize

TEXT CASE

uppercase

Set your title text case only if necessary

Use the `text-transform` property to set the text case to either lowercase or uppercase. You can also set `capitalize`, which will capitalize the first letter in each word.

```
text-transform: capitalize;
```

Adding this to all headers may seem like a good idea to ensure that they are properly formatted. Unfortunately, `capitalize` is applied indiscriminately to the text, meaning that certain words that should not be capitalized (of, the, etc.) will be capitalized anyway.

Use small caps for special emphasis

Although often maligned by designers, when used well, small caps (sometimes called *mini-caps*) can add nice emphasis to text more subtly than bold or italics can. `small-caps` will render all upper- and lowercase-letters as uppercase characters, but reduce the lowercase letters' height to the font's x-height:

```
font-variant: small-caps;
    text-sapcing: .05em;
```

When using small caps, it's also a good idea to loosen the letterspacing some by adding a small amount of tracking.

Small Caps of Distinction

jontangerine.com

Jon Tangerine's Web site (detail shown) combines small caps with a bottom border in his hypertext links to give them a distinctive look.

Axiom Axiom   x-height

roman   small caps

While the overuse of small caps can quickly become annoying, using them for special cases can add nice layer of texture to your typography.

COLOR

Color Intensity • The color saturation or color variance from pure white.

The most primal response we have to visual stimuli is our response to color. We associate colors with an ever-shifting series of feelings and concepts, including the religious, cultural, political, social, emotional, and scientific. Yet, despite this instinctual understanding of the meaning of colors—or possibly because of it—color proves elusively difficult to use in design effectively.

The challenge that designers at all levels face is not just knowing which colors work best together, but also knowing how to restrain themselves. The first lesson I learned in color theory class was: "No color is better than bad color."

Color values

Table 5.2 Color Values

Hex is the dominant method for declaring color values, but the new RGBA format will be a better choice when it is more widely available.

As explained in Chapter 4, "Scale & Rhythm," the screen is a series of colored dots, or pixels. A pixel's color value is defined as a combination of the primary colors—red, green, and blue—at different brightnesses and intensities. Most modern screens can display millions of different colors, defined by the combinations of those primary colors.

format	name	what it is	example
#RRGGBB	Hex	Hexcode values in couplets (00–99,aa–ff)	#CC33FF or #C3F
rgb(R#,G#,B#)	RGB Numeric	Numeric values (0–255)	rgb(204,51,255)
rgb(R%,G%,B%)	RGB Percentage	Percentage values (0%–100%)	rgb(81%,15%,100%)
rgba(R,G,B,A)	RGB Alpha	Numeric or percentage values with alpha (transparency) value (0–1)	rgba(204,52,255,.5)
name		The name of the color	purple

Table 5.2 shows the different ways to specify a color, mostly by combining RGB values from darkest to lightest. A new color value type available in Safari and Firefox is the RGB Alpha value, which allows you to set the transparency of the color from 0 (clear) to 1 (opaque). However, RGBA does not work with hex color values. In Web typography, color is set in four places:

Color Brightness • The variation in a color from black.

⊙ **Color** affects only the text color.

```
color: rgb(204,51,255);
```

⊙ **Background color** sets the color of the background of the body or an element in the design. Backgrounds can also include images, where the colors can be solid or stochastic.

```
background-color:  rgb(204,51,255);
```

⊙ **Border** includes a color value.

```
border: 1px solid rgb(204,51,255);
```

⊙ **Text shadow**, explained earlier in this chapter, includes a color value.

```
text-shadow: -2px 2px 10px
    rgb(204,51,255);
```

Choosing your color palette

When considering color in typography, we have to stretch our consideration of the design from the individual glyphs that make up blocks of text to also consider how the text interacts with the elements around it—that is, images and backgrounds.

There are several tried and true methods for combining colors that work consistently. You can identify them by their position on a color wheel.

◉ **Analogous**: Matching colors with adjacent hues.

◉ **Monochromatic**: A single color with varied intensity and brightnesses. This is the simplest to use well, and is recommended if you are unsure of how to work with color.

◉ **Triad**: Three colors and their tones, separated in a triangular shape in the color wheel.

◉ **Complementary**: Two colors from opposite sides of the color wheel, providing the highest contrast of any of the combinations.

◉ **Shades**: Multiple brightnesses of the same color.

A color palette can include only a single color, but more than five colors will tend to become overwhelming. Black and white are generally considered a part of every color palette, even if not explicitly included.

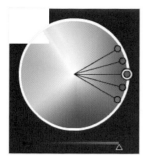

Analogous

Monochromatic

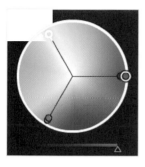

Triad

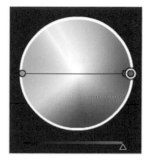

Complementary

Adobe Kuler

kuler.adobe.com

Choose the best color combination using the Kuler tool, set for analogous, monochromatic, triad, complementary, or shades.

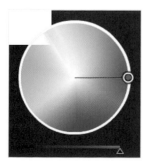

Shades

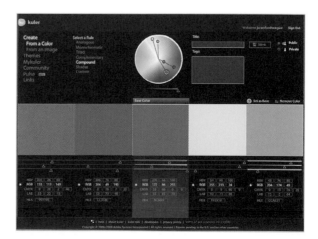

Consider contrast between foreground and background color carefully

The accepted standard when setting type and background colors is to maximize contrast to improve readability. Obviously, the colors that contrast most highly are black and white, which explains why so much type is set as black on a white background. Text is often set as white on black on the screen, where considerations like the price of ink are not relevant as they are in print. However, high contrast also tends to tire the eye over extended periods of time.

◉ One way to soften the tone of your pages and ease eyestrain is to slightly reduce the text contrast.

Soften Contrast
Use lower-contrasting colors against each other to soften your page and reduce eyestrain.

- Use lower-contrast text colors to de-emphasize elements such as menus, article bylines, dates, and other noncritical information, to help focus attention on the primary text and improve scanability.

De-emphasize Secondary Elements

FORMationalliance.com

The FORMation Web site (detail shown) uses light gray for a list of links to help focus attention on the primary content.

- Avoid background images with highly contrasting colors—for example, a photograph with strong areas of dark and light. It's not impossible to design against this type of background, but it generally proves to be a challenge to create and a challenge for readability.

No Noisy Backgrounds
A background where the colors strongly shift in contrast can prove to be challenging to design against, and even harder to read against.

Type Inspirations

Acid Smile

Typographically Innovative Blog and Portfolio

acidsmile.co.uk

Maria Theodoropoulou describes herself as a Greek geek living in the UK and working for Bluestorm design. Her site contains a basic blog and portfolio, but the types being used are not the common core Web fonts. Her design mixes rich textures and colors with text on photorealistic papers to create an inviting Web environment.

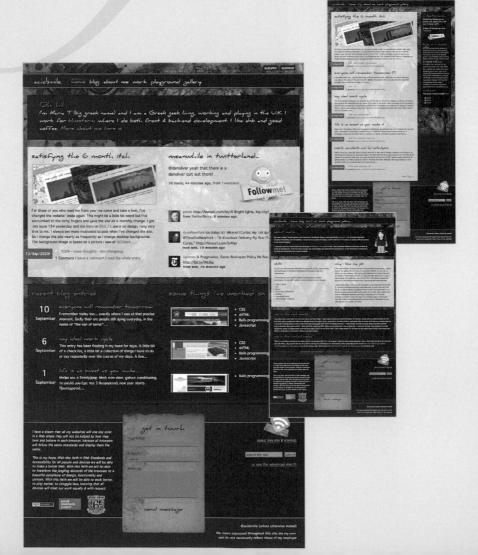

How they do it:

Acid Smile uses the Web font technology Cufón (explained in Chapter 3) to load the font Daniel as JavaScript data, which the page then uses liberally throughout with a variety of colors and sizes for headline treatments and callout text.

[THE GRID] IS A TOOL FOR CREATING ORDER, AND CREATING ORDER IS TYPOGRAPHY.

Wim Crouwel
Helvetica

GRID & COMPOSITION

Layout of text in a regular sequence aids the reader's comprehension of the page. Design to scale, establish a hierarchy, and choose the right typefaces to establish a strong typographic voice.

DO NOT DESIGN BY DEFAULT

When you talk, you modulate the tone of voice for different audiences. Your voice and cadence alter depending on whom you are speaking to. If you are talking to your boss, your voice (hopefully) sounds very different than if you were talking to your lover, even if the words are the same. Whether you adjust your voice to be formal, informal, humorous, serious, sensuous, or angry, it informs your audience about the meaning of your words.

Many Web designers allow the default values imposed by the browsers or by perceived limitations to dictate the voice of their designs, which

Scale • A sequence that helps preserve hierarchy and harmony when applied to a design.

LOOKING GLASS

BUS

dictate the scale and rhythm, and usually not well. It's like talking to everybody you know in exactly the same voice. Like a robot.

Reset the browser defaults and set your own global styles

Although there is some technical debate over exactly how you should reset styles and which styles should be reset, as a designer, I recommend resetting all typographic and spacing styles and then setting your own defaults. Don't let the browser determine your page styles. Another good argument for resetting styles is that different browsers have slightly different values, especially for margins, padding, and font sizes; and some browsers include borders where others may not. Resetting the styles gives all of the browsers the same baseline.

The easiest way to reset styles is with the universal selector. Set the default styles you want applied to all tags:

```
* { margin: 0;
    padding: 0;
    border: 0;
    outline: 0;
    font-size: 100%;
    vertical-align: baseline;
    text-decoration: none;
    background: transparent; }
```

This is a nice, quick way to get the most important styles reset, but it has one drawback: Microsoft Internet Explorer 6 does not recognize the universal selector. If you are concerned about supporting IE6, then you will want to include all of the HTML tags in the selector list. The advantage of using the universal selector is that it will always apply itself to new HTML tags as they become available.

Compose with a scale to create a typographical hierarchy

When scanning a Web page for information, the human eye looks for areas of contrast and areas of consistency. Too much consistency leads to a monotonous design, while too much contrast leads to chaotic noise. One way to balance contrast and consistency is to create a regular typographical hierarchy, where type fluidly scales from the top level (level 1 heading) into the body content (paragraphs).

§ For Web typography, the easiest way to implement a consistent scale is to use the em. Ems, as explained in Chapter 4, "Scale & Rhythm," are the basic units of typography, based on the current size of the font.

The scale you choose is up to you, but keep it consistent and easy to remember. You may want to scale based on doubling 2s (2, 4, 8, 16) or multiples of 3 (3, 6, 9, 12, 15) or multiples of 5 (5, 10, 15, 20). These values should inform not only your font sizes, but margins, padding, and widths, as well. Applying ems to scale allows you to create a relative scale that can then be controlled at the top level by setting the font size in the body tag.

One issue to overcome is the inconsistencies that browsers have in resizing fonts relatively. Some fonts exaggerate the size changes more than others, as shown in *Table 4.3*. One way to alleviate this issue is simply to set the font size of the body tag to 100%, which indicates that all tags should base their relative size on the browser's default font size.

```
body { font-size: 100%; }
```

Let's assume a default font size of 16px (the default on most browsers) when you want a paragraph font size of 12px. You can quickly create a scale, simple by using ems to scale the base font size up or down. For lower-level headers, which are rarely used, you can use different   styles, weights, or capitalization to differentiate them in the hierarchy.

```
h1 { font-size: 2em;    }
h2 { font-size: 1.5em;  }
h3 { font-size: 1.125em;  }
h4 { font-size: 1em;  }
h5, h6 { font-size: .875em;  }
h6 { font-style: italic; }
p, li, q, blockquote  {
   font-size: .75em;    }
```

body font size = 16px

2em = 32px

Level 1 Heading – h1

1.5em = 24px

Level 2 Heading – h2

1.125em = 18px

Level 3 Heading – h3

1em = 16px

Level 4 Heading – H4

.875em = 14px

Level 5 Heading – h5

.875em = 14px
italic

Level 6 Heading – h6

.75em = 12px

Paragraph - p. So Alice picked him up very gently, and lifted him across more slowly than she had lifted the Queen, that she mightn't take his breath away: but, before she put him on the table, she thought she might as well dust him a little, he was so covered with ashes.

Make links clear, not cluttered

The default style for hypertext links on the Web is underlined, so this is the style that readers have become accustomed to scanning for. Unfortunately, underlines do not contrast with the text, so they add visual noise to the very elements they are meant to highlight. Additionally, since not all links are created equal, underlining all links—even those in navigation and controls—diminishes the overall typographic contrast of your page.

Looking Glass   underline

Looking Glass   **border-bottom**
link

There is a better way to underline links than using the underline style. Adding a border to the bottom of a link gives you an underline that you can style. Start by turning underlining off in all links on your page:

Looking Glass   visited

Looking Glass   hover

Looking Glass   active

```
a { color: rgb(0,0,255);
    text-decoration: none; }
```

If you really need a link type to be underlined—for example, links in paragraphs—add it back on a case-by-case basis, using the `border-bottom` property instead of underline. This lets you create a controlled underline with different colors and styles:

```
p a:line { border-bottom: 1px solid rgb(153,153,255); }
p a:visited { border-bottom: 1px solid rgb(204,204,255); }
p a:link { border-bottom: 1px dotted rgb(153,153,255); }
p a:active { border-bottom: 1px solid rgb(255,0,0); }
```

HTML 5 AND THE FUTURE OF WEB TYPOGRAPHY

In June 2003, what would eventually become HTML 5 started life as Web Applications 1.0. It was created by the Web Hypertext Application Technology Working Group (WHATWG), which was not associated with the W3C at the time. Instead, this independent group, frustrated with the pace and direction that XHTML was taking, worked on an alternative that would not only be backward compatible, but also address many of the practical issues Web developers face.

Generally, CSS is associated with typography, since it is used to style text. However, HTML also has an important role to play in structuring the content that is then styled by CSS code. HTML 5 provides a more *semantic* markup, allowing designers to better segregate the content of their page to style elements individually.

HTML 5 makes important structural changes to Web pages—for example, allowing you to specify common elements such as headers, footers, articles, and asides. In addition, HTML 5 brings us many features natively (that is, built into the browser) that used to require plug-ins and/or scripting:

- Application Programming Interfaces (APIs) that allow developers to add interactivity more easily

- The canvas tag, which allows scriptable bitmap editing

- Document editing

- Web forms that self-validate and include more input types

- Drag and drop of elements without scripting

- Timed media playback

There is no escaping that HTML 5 is where Web design and development is headed. Many browsers have already started supporting some of its features, even though it's not a standard yet. That said, one notable curmudgeon on support (as it always seems to be) is Internet Explorer. Microsoft is at least reviewing the standard, however, and hope springs eternal.

For more information, check out the article I wrote on ways to start using HTML 5 now (*http://www.peachpit.com/blogs/blog.aspx?uk=HTML-5-NOW*).

FROM BOX TO GRID

Grids are a time-honored method for achieving regular structure and consistency within a Web page
and between pages on a Web site. For typography,
the grid becomes important when considering the
right font sizes for the space available. As mentioned
in Chapter 4, readability is partially dependent on
not allowing columns to stretch too wide or con-
dense too small.

For Web design, the grid is not only useful, but
it is the default way the page is structured. While
print designers can easily create elements of any
two-dimensional shape, every element in a Web
page created using HTML tags has an intrinsic box
around it. Although non-rectangular shapes can be
placed within, the basic element shape is always a
rectangle. These rectangular boxes naturally lend
themselves to creating solid layout grids.

Web design presents a problem not encountered in print, though, because the exact location
where the content will be displayed is unpredict-
able. Most Web designers attempt to define a fixed
width for columns, but as screens grow larger, it is
more and more imperative for designs to adapt to
this variable environment.

Structure your page by use

There are a variety of methods for structuring a
Web page grid, but given that HTML 5 will soon
become the default markup language, I recommend mirroring its nomenclature, even if we can't
use its exact code yet. One of the most significant
improvements over previous markup languages is

the addition of new structural elements that will greatly enhance the semantic philosophy behind Web markup. Here's a quick run-down:

◉ **Header**: Pretty obvious, but can be used for page headers, section headers, article headers, or an aside header.

◉ **Navigation**: Could be included independently or as part of the header and/or footer.

◉ **Section**: Defines the main parts of the page, generally containing articles.

◉ **Article**: An individual blog entry or blog entry abstract.

◉ **Aside**: Used for support content on a page, such as related links, secondary navigation, and, of course, ads.

◉ **Footer**: Similar to the header, it can be placed at the bottom of other elements.

Begin your grid by adding HTML tags with classes that identify the various sectors of your layout grid by their use within the design. I also recommend adding a surrounding parent element called **page**, to control the overall width of the content area.

Once your basic structure is in place, you will use CSS to set your page and column widths, using either a fixed width for precise widths or a variable width for fluid widths.

§ The width of your columns is an important factor in the readability of your page. You don't want them too wide or too narrow, as explained in Chapter 4.

```
<html>
<head><title>FWT</title></head>
<body>
</div id="page">
<div class="header">
<div class="navigation"></div>
</div>
<div class="section">
<div class="article">
<div class="header"></div>
</div>
<div class="article">
<div class="header"></div>
</div>
</div>
<div class="aside"></div>
<div class="footer"></div>
</div>
</body></html>
```

Structure Your Page

The HTML to structure a basic three-column grid design with header and footer.

The layout below shows a likely configuration of this structure, once the aside and section elements are floated next to each other to create columns.

Use fixed width for a precise grid

Most Web designs use a fixed-width page, generally centered in the browser window. Although standards have changed over the years, a content area width of 920px–980px is considered standard today, assuming that the majority of monitors have a width of 1024px or more. This gives comfortable spacing for most (but not all) people reading the page.

To create a fixed page width, set the width in the **page** selector to the desired length. We'll use 960px as an example. You could then calculate exact pixel widths for each column based on the formula presented in Chapter 4, but I recommend setting column widths for the **section** and **aside** classes as percentages (including a percentage margin on section), as this will allow you to change the **page** width without having to recalculate the column widths:

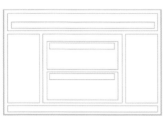

Fixed-Width Columns

Regardless of the browser window width, the columns stay the same width.

```
.page {  width: 960px;
         margin: 10px auto; }
.section {  float: left;
            width: 50%;
            margin: 0 1.6%; }
.aside { float: left;
         width: 23.25%; }
```

The aside columns will be about 224px, the central section column will be 480px, and the gutter between will be about 15px. Notice that this only adds up to 958px, leaving an extra 2 pixels unaccounted for. These will be to the right of the page. I find it's good to leave a few pixels of breathing room in the design to allow for rounding errors and browser quirks. I've also added the auto margin to center the page.

Use variable widths for fluid grids

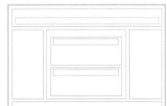

Although fixed widths are all the rage, consider an alternative—using CSS to create a column width range. Although a screen size of 1024px is currently considered to be the average size, there are plenty of readers who may still have smaller screens and many more who simply do not browse with their browsers open to full screen.

    I would never recommend allowing columns to stretch unimpeded across an entire screen. After a point, the width will reduce the readability of your text. Likewise, columns can only get so thin before they become useless for reading text. Then a horizontal scroll would actually be preferred. However, there is a wide range of widths between these two extremes.

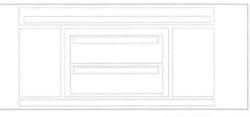

Fluid-Width Columns

The columns will stretch to best fill the browser window, but only to a point, beyond which it stays fixed.

For optimal reading, use a base font size of 16px, with a range in size for the central column somewhere between 400px (16 × 25) and around 530px (16 × 33). Since the central column is half the width of the page, we need to multiply this by a factor of two to set the width of the full page, giving us a range of 800px to 1060px—a healthy range. To set this range, we will rely on the min/max CSS properties:

```
.page {  min-width: 800px;
         max-width: 1060px;
         _width: 920px;
         padding: 0 1.5%;
         margin: 10px auto; }
.section {  float: left;
            width: 50%;
            margin: 0 1.6%; }
.aside { float: left;
         width: 23.25%; }
```

The page will now stretch and contract to optimize to the reader's screen, without diminishing the readability. This code also accommodates Internet Explorer 6, which does not recognize the min/max properties, giving a fixed width of 920px for it. Adding a fixed width with an underscore before it, as I have in line three of the code, is a quick hack to make sure that only IE6 sees the code it needs.

Fluid Layout in Use

Amazon.com uses a fluid center column, allowing them to show more products to visitors with larger screens.

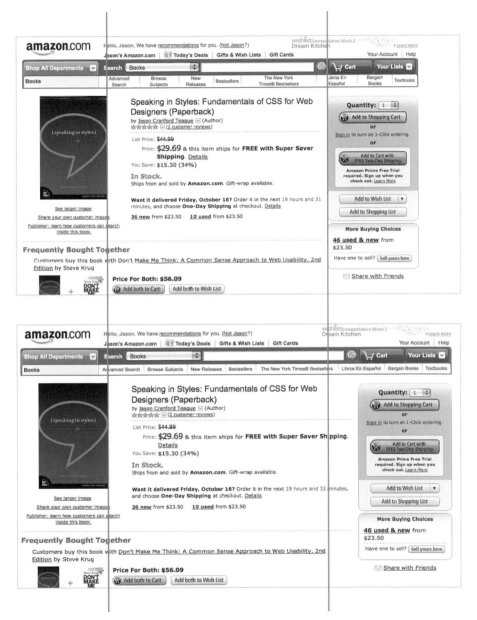

CHOOSING THE RIGHT TYPEFACE

What is the font's voice?

My perceptions of a few fonts. What's your reaction to these fonts?

Looking Glass

Times—*Trustworthy but dull*

Looking Glass

Fontin—*Elegant and restrained*

LOOKING GLASS

Fresh—*Retro future*

looking Glass

Acidreflux—*Nervous and scared*

Looking Glass

TRASHED—*Grungy and corrupted*

Looking Glass

Trebuchet MS—*Efficient and techy*

Looking Glass

Mistral—*Casual and fun*

Looking Glass

Cooper Black—*Big and friendly*

Looking Glass

Arial—*Clean but dull*

When you only had ten fonts, choosing one from this list was easy. Now that you have dozens of Web safe fonts and can link to any font that is licensed for Web downloading, your horizons are much broader. This new power, though, comes with the responsibility of having to be thoughtful in your choices. The exact type you choose should depend on several factors.

Establish a typographic voice

Choose your typeface to reflect the mood and demeanor of the message your Web site is conveying. If the site is meant to be upbeat and happy, choose fonts with a playful look. If the site is meant to be professional and serious, choose clean, simple fonts.

I once worked with a writer who published a daily advice column. She insisted, despite my protests, on publishing her column in Comic Sans MS, a font that is generally ridiculed by typographers. I quickly realized that this font "spoke" to her audience in a relaxed, informal tone that no other available font could have achieved. She was actually using the typeface to better communicate her message.

We now have a wide selection of fonts to choose from, so choose those that best serve the content's message. It's important that you define the voice you are trying to achieve, and then choose typefaces accordingly.

Use the right fonts in the right places

With ready access to more than just a handful of fonts, it is tempting to use more than we need. If we aren't careful, we will see an explosion of bad typography. Something similar happened early in Web design. Designers, used to the color limitations in print, went a little overboard when they could use any and all colors in a single design. It is important with Web typography, as with any design, always to have a purpose for your typeface choices.

In this book, for example, I wanted to create a balance between the past and the future. All body copy is set in the Perpetua font family, which is also a Web safe font. Titles and auxiliary content—such as captions and sidebars—are set in the sans-serif typeface Museo, a free font you can use with `@font-linking` in a Web page. I chose these fonts because not only do they look good together—contrasting serif and sans serif—but I also wanted to put my money where my mouth is by using typefaces that can be set both in print and in Web sites. The one typeface exception I made was for text used to display computer code, which is traditionally monospace, so I used Consolas.

If you are new to typography or design, limit yourself to a single font, leveraging its weights and styles and varying colors to create contrast.

What is this book's typographic voice?

My perceptions of the fonts I chose for this book.

Looking Glass

Museo Sans—*Clean and futuristic*

Looking Glass

Perpetua—*Classic but fun*

Looking Glass

Consolas—*Technical*

BUILDING A FLUID FONT STACK

In Chapter 3, "Fonts & Typefaces," we explored the many ways to find typefaces for use in your Web designs. One of the prime tenets of fluid Web typography, though, is that things change, and you cannot assume that the first font you choose is the one in which the end user reads your text. Many variables can contribute to this uncertainty, but the solution is to be prepared, by creating a fluid font stack with backup fonts.

It is important, however, when putting the font stack together to choose fonts that not only look similar but behave similarly on the page. Here are a few of the most important considerations.

Find screen-friendly fonts for body copy

Although you may have a candy store of fonts to choose from now, some are more legible at body copy sizes (16px or below) than others. Two factors to consider with the legibility of a font are its x-height and letterspacing. A font with a taller x-height will generally be easier to read on the screen. Additionally, if you can find fonts whose characters are slightly spaced apart, they will not clash with each other on the screen. If you need to, add a small amount of letterspacing or word spacing to headlines or body text:

```
h1, h2, h3, h4, h5, h6
    { word-spacing: .1em; }
p   { letter-spacing: .03em }
```

Use fonts with similar widths and kerning

Because headlines generally have a confined height—you don't want the headline to take up more than a certain horizontal space in the design—choosing fonts with similar widths will ensure that one font will not take up much more space if used than any of the fallbacks.

Body copy may need to occupy a specific column width for readability, so choosing typefaces with widths and kerning will ensure that one does not take more vertical space than any of the alternatives.

Test your fonts, by placing them one after another and comparing lengths (for headlines) and heights (for body copy). There is a certain amount of variation that can occur, but you don't want any font to be off from the others by more than 2em over the width of the line.

Looking Glass   diavlo

Looking Glass   tahoma

Looking Glass   arial

One thing was certain, that the *white* kitten had had nothing to do with it:—it was the black kitten's fault entirely. For the white kitten had been having its face washed by the old cat for the last quarter of an hour (and bearing it pretty well, considering); so you see that it *couldn't* have had any hand in the mischief.

bell mt

One thing was certain, that the *white* kitten had had nothing to do with it:—it was the black kitten's fault entirely. For the white kitten had been having its face washed by the old cat for the last quarter of an hour (and bearing it pretty well, considering); so you see that it *couldn't* have had any hand in the mischief.

garamond

One thing was certain, that the *white* kitten had had nothing to do with it:—it was the black kitten's fault entirely. For the white kitten had been having its face washed by the old cat for the last quarter of an hour (and bearing it pretty well, considering); so you see that it *couldn't* have had any hand in the mischief.

times

Make sure that a typeface includes all of the weights and styles you need

Although there are ways to style around it, you should make sure that if you are using the bold, italics, and/or oblique versions of a typeface in your design, the typeface supports these styles. Otherwise, the browser will likely synthesize them, which rarely looks good.

One way around this is to specify different typefaces or different styles rather than bold or italics. For example, rather than using a heavier font for the bold or strong tags, you could set `font-weight` to normal and use all caps or `small-caps`:

```
b, strong {
  font-weight: normal;
  font-variant: small-caps;  }
```

Use this technique sparingly, as it can create a strong typographic voice that may not be desired.

Download fonts as needed, but consider download times

Although downloading fonts allows you to add typefaces without images, you are still downloading files, which can slow down your Web site. Check the list of Web safe fonts first to see if one of those meets your needs before resorting to the download. However, you will always want to put your linked fonts first, since whether you use them or not, the file is still downloaded.

Include Web safe, core, and generic font-family backups

Include a list of multiple fonts, starting with linked fonts, then Web safe fonts, then core Web fonts, and finally a generic font family. This will ensure that the fonts you most want to be used are tried first, and then the fallbacks are tried, all the way down to the default generic font that the browser has on hand. Obviously, you can include as many different font families of each type as desired.

```
                 web safe                     core    generic
                    |                          |       |
                    |                          |       |
  body {            |                          |       |
    font-family: "bell mt","goudy old style",times,serif; }
  h1, h2, h3, h4, h5, h6 {
    font-family: "alice headline",tahoma,arial,sans-serif; }
                    |              |       |      |
                    |              |       |      |
                  linked       web safe  core  generic
```

APPENDIXES

COLOPHON

HARDWARE & OS

Written and produced on an iMac and MacBook Air using Mac OS 10.5 and 10.6. Testing for Windows done with Crossover. Additional testing and Windows font cards produced using VMWare Fusion running Windows Vista and a Dell Dimension 8300 running Windows Vista Business.

SOFTWARE

- ◉ **Outlining**–OmniOutliner

- ◉ **Writing**–Scrivener

- ◉ **Coding**–Panic Coda

- ◉ **Composition**–Adobe InDesign

- ◉ **Illustration**–Adobe Illustrator

- ◉ **Additional Illustration**–OmniGraffle

- ◉ **Editing**–Adobe Acrobat Professional

TYPEFACES

This book's body copy is set in Perpetua, titles set in Museo and Museo Sans, and computer code set in Consolas. Additional fonts were used in the book for illustrations and examples.

All font samples presented in 14pt for size comparison.

Looking Glass

Acid Reflux

© Copyright 2002 CHANK/Pennyzine. All rights reserved. Do not redistribute this font without persmission. By Jason Ramirez for Chank.com and pennyzine.com. Good Luck!

Looking Glass

Arial

Designers Monotype Type Drawing Office - Robin Nicholas, Patricia Saunders 1982
© 2006 The Monotype Corporation. All Rights Reserved.

Looking Glass

Bickham Script Pro

Designer Richard Lipton
© 1997, 1998, 1999, 2004 Adobe Systems Incorporated. All Rights Reserved.

Looking Glass

Consolas

Designer Luc(as) de Groot
© 2005 Microsoft Corporation. All Rights Reserved.

Looking Glass

Cooper Black

Data copyright © URW Software & Type GmbH., additional data copyright The Monotype Corporation. Copyright 1994 Microsoft Corporation. All rights reserved.

Looking Glass

Courier

© 1989, 1990, 1991, 1992, 1993, 1996, 1997, 1998 Adobe Systems Incorporated. All Rights Reserved.

Looking Glass

Cracked

© 1993 House Industries, Brand Design Company. Copyright © 2001, 2006 Apple Computer, Inc. All rights reserved.

Looking Glass

Fontin Sans

Designer Jos Buivenga
© 2007 by Jos Buivenga. All rights reserved.

Looking Glass

Franklin Gothic Book

Designer Victor Caruso
ITC Franklin Gothic is a trademark of The International Typeface Corporation which may be registered in certain jurisdictions. Portions copyright Microsoft Corporation. All rights reserved.

Looking Glass

Fresh

© Copyright 2002 CHANK/Fontalicious Fonts. All Rights Reserved. Do not redistribute this font. Fontalicious is a registered trademark of Globitron, Inc. www.fontalicious.com www.chank.com

Looking Glass

Garamond

Digitized data copyright Monotype Typography, Ltd 1991-1995. All rights reserved. Monotype Garamond® is a trademark of Monotype Typography, Ltd which may be registered in certain jurisdictions.

Looking Glass

Georgia

Designer Matthew Carter
© 2006 Microsoft Corporation. All Rights Reserved.

Looking Glass

Helvetica

© 1990-2006 Apple Computer Inc. © 1981 Linotype AG © 1990 91 Type Solutions Inc.

Looking Glass

Helvetica Neue

Designer Linotype Design Studio
Part of the digitally encoded machine readable outline data for producing the Typefaces provided is copyrighted © 2003 – 2006 Linotype GmbH, www.linotype.com. All rights reserved. This software is the property of Linotype GmbH, and may not be reproduced, modified, disclosed or transferred without the express written approval of Linotype GmbH. Copyright © 1988, 1990, 1993 Adobe Systems Incorporated. All Rights Reserved. Helvetica is a trademark of Heidelberger Druckmaschinen AG, exclusively licensed through Linotype GmbH, and may be registered in certain jurisdictions. This typeface is original artwork of Linotype Design Studio. The design may be protected in certain jurisdictions.

Looking Glass

Mistral

© Copyright by URW, 1992. Portions © 1992 Microsoft Corp. All rights reserved.

Looking Glass

Modern No. 20

Data by Anna Wheeler and Type Solutions, Inc. © 1993. Microsoft Corporation. All rights reserved.

Looking Glass

Museo

Designer Jos Buivenga
© 2008 by Jos Buivenga. All rights reserved.

Looking Glass

Museo Sans

Designer Jos Buivenga
© 2007 by Jos Buivenga. All rights reserved.

LOOKING GLASS

NoMak

© Copyright 2008 Chank Co. All rights reserved. Do not redistribute without permission.

Looking Glass

Palatino

© 1991-99, 2006 Apple Computer, Inc. Copyright © 1991-92 Type Solutions, Inc. All rights reserved.

Looking Glass

Perpetua

Designer Eric Gill
Digitized data copyright The Monotype Corporation 1991-1995. All rights reserved. Perpetua® is a trademark of The Monotype Corporation which may be registered in certain jurisdictions.

Looking Glass

Rockwell

Digitized data copyright © 1992 - 1997 The Monotype Corporation. Rockwell ® is a trademark of The Monotype Corporation which may be registered in certain jurisdictions. Portions copyright Microsoft Corporation. All rights reserved.

LOOKING GLASS

Rosewood Std

Designers Kim Buker Chansler, Carl Crossgrove, Carol Twombly
© 1993, 1994, 2001 Adobe Systems Incorporated. All Rights Reserved.

Looking Glass

Snell Roundhand

© 1990 Linotype AG, © 2001 Apple Computer, Inc.

LOOKING GLASS

Synchro LET

© 1990 Esselte Letraset, Ltd. All rights reserved.

Looking Glass

Times

© 1990-99 Apple Computer Inc. © 1981 Linotype AG © 1990-91 Type Solutions Inc. © 1990-91 The Font Bureau Inc.

Looking Glass

TRASHED

Last Soundtrack (Guillaume Séguin) // lastsoundtrack.com

Looking Glass

Trebuchet MS

Designer Vincent Connare
Copyright © 1996 Microsoft Corporation. All rights reserved.

Looking Glass

Verdana

Typeface and data © 1996 Microsoft Corporation. All Rights
Reserved

TYPOGRAPHY RESOURCES

APPENDIX

Over the course of researching and writing this book, I consulted a lot of different Web sites, magazines, and books. Some are quite well known, while others are well off the beaten path. While I cannot list all of them here, I wanted to list some of my favorites, especially those that may not be as well known as others.

I will also be regularly updating this list, and reviewing Web typography sites, on *fluidwebtype.info*.

THE AUTHOR'S WEB SITES

Speaking In Styles | *speakinginstyles.com*

My own Web site, where I regularly rant about the balance between technology and design.

Fluid Web Type | *fluidwebtype.info*

The support Web site for this book, where you can find samples, updates, errata, and Web typography resources.

TOOLS

Em Calculator | *typetester.org*

Calculate relative em sizes based on your desired pixel size to create fluid design.

TypeTester | *triddle.pl/emcalc*

Preview and compare different Web safe fonts. Excellent for finding fonts with similar heights that look good on the screen.

Fontstruct | *fontstruct.fontshop.com/*

Build and share your own fonts in an easy-to-use online environment.

The 1Kb CSS Grid | *1kbgrid.com*

Choose the number of columns, the column width, and the gutter width; click a button; and download CSS and HTML code for your fixed-width grid. And the font size is only 1 Kb.

html-ipsum.com | *1kbgrid.com*

A simple site with easy-to-grab lorem ipsum code for a variety of needs, like paragraphs, lists, forms, and tables.

CSS Text Wrapper | *csstextwrap.com*

Use CSS or JavaScript to break the rectangular grid with angles, curves, and even circles.

CSS Web-Typography Matrix and code generator | *www.jan-quickels.de/tools-web-typography*

Enter your font sizes in pixels to generate the font, size, line height, and optimum margins in ems along with CSS to implement them.

FONT DOWNLOADS

Fonts.info | *fonts.info*

Only a few fonts, but a few *great* fonts.

Font Squirrel | *fontsquirrel.com*

Lots and lots of fonts, all free for the taking and all available as kits for Web font linking. Go here often.

Font Fabric | *fontfabric.com*

Some beautiful fonts for free.

SIL International | *scripts.sil.org*

Where you can download the (free) Gentium font family, which is specifically designed for international use.

exljbris fonts | *fontstruct.fontshop.com/*

Some of my favorite free fonts, including Museo Sans, which is what you are reading in now.

Hype For Type | *hypefortype.com*

Use CSS or JavaScript to break the rectangular grid with angles, curves, and even circles.

Free Typography | *freetypography.com*

Find your free fonts here.

Typographica | *typographica.org*

A beautiful design that highlights the best in typography and the best new fonts.

Typophile | *typophile.com*

A community of type designers and typographers. If you have a question, post it here for a quick answer.

Smashing Magazine | *smashingmagazine.com*

Every day, I learn something new from this one. I especially recommend following their tweets (on Twitter, in case you didn't know).

Nice Web Type | *nicewebtype.com*

Highlights the best typography from around the Web.

I Love Typography | *ilovetypography.com*

Not just for typography fanatics, this site is all about typography.

Webdesigner Depot | *webdesignerdepot.com*

Web designers and developers read the articles here to find ideas for all aspects of Web design.

Fuel Your Creativity | *fuelyourcreativity.com*

If you need inspiration with a practical twist, this is the best source.

Web Fonts | *webfonts.info*

A wiki devoted to Web typography and @font-face font embedding.

The Elements of Typographic Style Applied to the Web | *webtypography.net*

An update (although not written by the original author) to the wonderful book *The Elements of Typographic Style*.

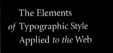

Association Typographique Internationale | *atypi.org*

A place to learn about type and commune with typographers.

Information Architects | *informationarchitects.jp*

Some of the best thoughts on Web design and Web typography there are to be found.

The Grid System | *thegridsystem.org*

For more information on the power of designing to a grid, there is no better site.

Ban Helvetica | *banhelvetica.com*

A funny little site that wants to promote the use of fonts like Comic Sans in place of Helvetica. It's a joke. I **hope** it's a joke.

Clagnut | *clagnut.com*

The home of Web designer Richard Rutter, who always has something interesting to say.

BOOKS & MAGAZINES

The Elements of Typographic Style | *Robert Bringhurst*

The book on typography. Bringhurst writes in a way that is both deep and wide, with excellent examples and practical advice.

Stop Stealing Sheep & Find Out How Type Works | *Eric Speakerman*

An incredible little book with a funny title. This book teaches typography as a visual and textual narrative rather than dry rules.

The Complete Manual of Typography | *James Felici*

Complete, thorough, and excellent text, especially for teaching typographic design.

Thinking with Type | *Ellen Lupton*

An inspirational and informative guide to typography, chock full of examples and beautiful type.

The Non-Designer's Type Book | *Robin Williams*

Robin Williams taught me the first thing I ever learned about type on the screen—never double-space after a period. Her books are a must-read.

Step Inside Design | *stepinsidedesign.com*

Bringing together some of the best design thinkers from around the world, this magazine never fails to provoke thought.

.net Magazine | *netmag.co.uk*

The best all-around Web designer's mag, *.net Magazine* has everything that code-savvy Web designers need to stay on top of their game.

CHARACTER REFERENCES

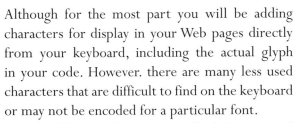

APPENDIX

Although for the most part you will be adding characters for display in your Web pages directly from your keyboard, including the actual glyph in your code. However. there are many less used characters that are difficult to find on the keyboard or may not be encoded for a particular font.

The following list presents all of these special characters, and code that can be used to include them in any HTML page, without having to type the character glyph directly into your HTML. The code can either be entered as an HTML character entity reference or Unicode code point.

Which set you use will depend on your needs, although I generally find the HTML references much easier to remember. If you do choose Unicode references, make sure to set your page encoding to a version of UTF, as explained in chapter 2.

Chapter 2 highlights many commonly misused characters that should be set using character references.

HTML	Unicode	Glyph	Description
&lsquo;		'	left single quote
&rsquo;		'	right single quote
&sbquo;		‚	single low-9 quote
&ldquo;		"	left double quote
&rdquo;		"	right double quote
&bdquo;		„	double low-9 quote
&dagger;		†	dagger
&Dagger;		‡	double dagger
&permil;		‰	per mill sign
&lsaquo;		‹	single left-pointing angle quote
&rsaquo;		›	single right-pointing angle quote
&spades;		♠	black spade suit
&clubs;		♣	black club suit
&hearts;		♥	black heart suit
&diams;		♦	black diamond suit
&oline;		‾	overline
&larr;		←	leftward arrow
&uarr;		↑	upward arrow
&rarr;		→	rightward arrow
&darr;		↓	downward arrow
&trade;		™	trademark sign
	&#09;		horizontal tab
	&#10;		line feed
	&#32;		space
	&#33;	!	exclamation mark
&quot;	&#34;	"	double quotation mark
	&#35;	#	number sign
	&#36;	$	dollar sign
	&#37;	%	percent sign
&amp;	&#38;	&	ampersand
	&#39;	'	apostrophe
	&#40;	(	left parenthesis

HTML	Unicode	Glyph	Description
	)	)	right parenthesis
	*	*	asterisk
	+	+	plus sign
	,	,	comma
	-	-	hyphen
	.	.	period
⁄	/	/	slash
	0 – 9		digits 0-9
	:	:	colon
	;	;	semicolon
<	<	<	less-than sign
	=	=	equals sign
>	>	>	greater-than sign
	?	?	question mark
	@	@	at sign
	A – Z		uppercase letters A-Z
	[	[	left square bracket
	\	\	backslash
	]	]	right square bracket
	^	^	caret
	_	_	underscore
	`	`	grave accent
	&#97 – z	a-z	lowercase letters a-z
	{	{	left curly brace
	|	|	vertical bar
	}	}	right curly brace
	~	~	tilde
–	–	–	en dash
—	—	—	em dash
			nonbreaking space
¡	¡	¡	inverted exclamation
¢	¢	¢	cent sign

HTML	Unicode	Glyph	Description
£	£	£	pound sterling
¤	¤	¤	general currency sign
¥	¥	¥	yen sign
&brkbar;	¦	¦	broken vertical bar
§	§	§	section sign
¨	¨	¨	umlaut
©	©	©	copyright
ª	ª	ª	feminine ordinal
«	«	«	left angle quote
¬	¬	¬	not sign
­	­		soft hyphen
®	®	®	registered trademark
¯	¯	¯	macron accent
°	°	°	degree sign
±	±	±	plus or minus
²	²	²	superscript two
³	³	³	superscript three
´	´	´	acute accent
µ	µ	µ	micro sign
¶	¶	¶	paragraph sign
·	·	·	middle dot
¸	¸	¸	cedilla
¹	¹	¹	superscript one
º	º	º	masculine ordinal
»	»	»	right angle quote
¼	¼	¼	one-fourth
½	½	½	one-half
¾	¾	¾	three-fourths
¿	¿	¿	inverted question mark
À	À	À	uppercase A, grave accent
Á	Á	Á	uppercase A, acute accent
Â	Â	Â	uppercase A, circumflex accent

HTML	Unicode	Glyph	Description
Ã	Ã	Ã	uppercase A, tilde
Ä	Ä	Ä	uppercase A, umlaut
Å	Å	Å	uppercase A, ring
Æ	Æ	Æ	uppercase AE
Ç	Ç	Ç	uppercase C, cedilla
È	È	È	uppercase E, grave accent
É	É	É	uppercase E, acute accent
Ê	Ê	Ê	uppercase E, circumflex accent
Ë	Ë	Ë	uppercase E, umlaut
Ì	Ì	Ì	uppercase I, grave accent
Í	Í	Í	uppercase I, acute accent
Î	Î	Î	uppercase I, circumflex accent
Ï	Ï	Ï	uppercase I, umlaut
Ð	Ð	Ð	uppercase Eth, Icelandic
Ñ	Ñ	Ñ	uppercase N, tilde
Ò	Ò	Ò	uppercase O, grave accent
Ó	Ó	Ó	uppercase O, acute accent
Ô	Ô	Ô	uppercase O, circumflex accent
Õ	Õ	Õ	uppercase O, tilde
Ö	Ö	Ö	uppercase O, umlaut
×	×	×	multiplication sign
Ø	Ø	Ø	uppercase O, slash
Ù	Ù	Ù	uppercase U, grave accent
Ú	Ú	Ú	uppercase U, acute accent
Û	Û	Û	uppercase U, circumflex accent
Ü	Ü	Ü	uppercase U, umlaut
Ý	Ý	Ý	uppercase Y, acute accent
Þ	Þ	Þ	uppercase THORN, Icelandic
ß	ß	ß	lowercase sharps, German
à	à	à	lowercase a, grave accent
á	á	á	lowercase a, acute accent
â	â	â	lowercase a, circumflex accent

HTML	Unicode	Glyph	Description
&atilde;	&#227;	ã	lowercase a, tilde
&auml;	&#228;	ä	lowercase a, umlaut
&aring;	&#229;	å	lowercase a, ring
&aelig;	&#230;	æ	lowercase ae
&ccedil;	&#231;	ç	lowercase c, cedilla
&egrave;	&#232;	è	lowercase e, grave accent
&eacute;	&#233;	é	lowercase e, acute accent
&ecirc;	&#234;	ê	lowercase e, circumflex accent
&euml;	&#235;	ë	lowercase e, umlaut
&igrave;	&#236;	ì	lowercase i, grave accent
&iacute;	&#237;	í	lowercase i, acute accent
&icirc;	&#238;	î	lowercase i, circumflex accent
&iuml;	&#239;	ï	lowercase i, umlaut
&eth;	&#240;	ð	lowercase eth, Icelandic
&ntilde;	&#241;	ñ	lowercase n, tilde
&ograve;	&#242;	ò	lowercase o, grave accent
&oacute;	&#243;	ó	lowercase o, acute accent
&ocirc;	&#244;	ô	lowercase o, circumflex accent
&otilde;	&#245;	õ	lowercase o, tilde
&ouml;	&#246;	ö	lowercase o, umlaut
&divide;	&#247;	÷	division sign
&oslash;	&#248;	ø	lowercase o, slash
&ugrave;	&#249;	ù	lowercase u, grave accent
&uacute;	&#250;	ú	lowercase u, acute accent
&ucirc;	&#251;	û	lowercase u, circumflex accent
&uuml;	&#252;	ü	lowercase u, umlaut
&yacute;	&#253;	ý	lowercase y, acute accent
&thorn;	&#254;	þ	lowercase thorn, Icelandic
&yuml;	&#255;	ÿ	lowercase y, umlaut

WEB FONT SPECIMEN BOOK

Although most Web sites only use the core Web fonts, there are actually dozens of fonts pre-installed on both Mac and Windows computers available for your Web designs, many of which are available on both platforms.

This appendix presents font samples of all of the typefaces likely to be pre-installed along with 30 free downloadable typefaces that are licensed for font linking as described in Chapter 3, "Fonts & Typefaces." The URL where you can download the file is included. Each card includes the font name, which can be used in a font stack; the weights and styles available; and where the typeface is available.

For more fonts, visit *fluidwebtype.info*.

availability

cross OS

mac

windows

linked

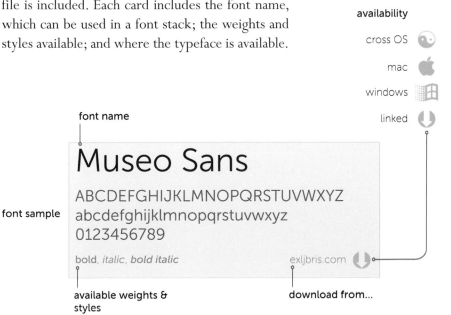

font name

Museo Sans

ABCDEFGHIJKLMNOPQRSTUVWXYZ
abcdefghijklmnopqrstuvwxyz
0123456789

font sample

bold, *italic*, *bold italic*

exljbris.com

available weights & styles

download from...

Academy Engraved LET

ABCDEFGHIJKLMNOPQRSTUVWXYZ
abcdefghijklmnopqrstuvwxyz
0123456789

Agency FB

ABCDEFGHIJKLMNOPQRSTUVWXYZ
abcdefghijklmnopqrstuvwxyz
0123456789

bold

ALGERIAN

ABCDEFGHIJKLMNOPQRSTUVWXYZ
0123456789

Aller

ABCDEFGHIJKLMNOPQRSTUVWXYZ
abcdefghijklmnopqrstuvwxyz
0123456789

bold, *italic*, *bold italic*   fontsquirrel.com

American Typewriter

ABCDEFGHIJKLMNOPQRSTUVWXYZ
abcdefghijklmnopqrstuvwxyz
0123456789

bold

Angelina

ABCDEFGHIJKLMNOPQRSTUVWXYZ
abcdefghijklmnopqrstuvwxyz
0123456789

fontsquirrel.com

Apple Chancery

ABCDEFGHIJKLMNOPQRSTUVWXYZ
abcdefghijklmnopqrstuvwxyz
0123456789

Aquiline

ABCDEFGHIJKLMNOPQRSTUVWXYZ
abcdefghijklmnopqrstuvwxyz
0123456789

fontsquirrel.com

Arial Narrow

ABCDEFGHIJKLMNOPQRSTUVWXYZ
abcdefghijklmnopqrstuvwxyz
0123456789

bold, *italic*, ***bold italic***

Arial Rounded MT

ABCDEFGHIJKLMNOPQRSTUVWXYZ
abcdefghijklmnopqrstuvwxyz
0123456789

Ballpark Weiner

ABCDEFGHIJKLMNOPQRSTUVWXYZ
abcdefghijklmnopqrstuvwxyz
0123456789

fontsquirrel.com

BANK GOTHIC

ABCDEFGHIJKLMNOPQRSTUVWXYZ
ABCDEFGHIJKLMNOPQRSTUVWXYZ
0123456789

Baskerville

ABCDEFGHIJKLMNOPQRSTUVWXYZ
abcdefghijklmnopqrstuvwxyz
0123456789

bold, *italic*, ***bold italic***

Baskerville Old Face

ABCDEFGHIJKLMNOPQRSTUVWXYZ
abcdefghijklmnopqrstuvwxyz
0123456789

Bauhaus 93

ABCDEFGHIJKLMNOPQRSTUVWXYZ
abcdefghijklmnopqrstuvwxyz
0123456789

Bell MT

ABCDEFGHIJKLMNOPQRSTUVWXYZ
abcdefghijklmnopqrstuvwxyz
0123456789

bold, *italic*

Berlin Sans FB

ABCDEFGHIJKLMNOPQRSTUVWXYZ
abcdefghijklmnopqrstuvwxyz
0123456789

bold

Berlin Sans FB Demi Bold

ABCDEFGHIJKLMNOPQRSTUVWXYZ
abcdefghijklmnopqrstuvwxyz
0123456789

Bernard MT Condensed

ABCDEFGHIJKLMNOPQRSTUVWXYZ
abcdefghijklmnopqrstuvwxyz
0123456789

Big Caslon

ABCDEFGHIJKLMNOPQRSTUVWXYZ
abcdefghijklmnopqrstuvwxyz
0123456789

Blackadder ITC
ABCDEFGHIJKLMNOPQRSTUVWXYZ
abcdefghijklmnopqrstuvwxyz
0123456789

BlackJackRegular
ABCDEFGHIJKLMNOPQRSTUVWXYZ
abcdefghijklmnopqrstuvwxyz
0123456789

fontsquirrel.com

Blackmoor LET
ABCDEFGHIJKLMNOPQRSTUVWXYZ
abcdefghijklmnopqrstuvwxyz
0123456789

BLACKOUT
ABCDEFGHIJKLMNOPQRSTUVWXYZ
ABCDEFGHIJKLMNOPQRSTUVWXYZ
0123456789

theleagueofmoveabletype.com

BLAIRMDITC TT
ABCDEFGHIJKLMNOPQRSTUVWXYZ
ABCDEFGHIJKLMNOPQRSTUVWXYZ
0123456789

Bodoni MT

ABCDEFGHIJKLMNOPQRSTUVWXYZ
abcdefghijklmnopqrstuvwxyz
0123456789

bold, *italic*, *bold italic*

Bodoni MT Condensed

ABCDEFGHIJKLMNOPQRSTUVWXYZ
abcdefghijklmnopqrstuvwxyz
0123456789

bold, *italic*, *bold italic*

Bodoni MT Poster Compressed

ABCDEFGHIJKLMNOPQRSTUVWXYZ
abcdefghijklmnopqrstuvwxyz
0123456789

Bodoni SvtyTwo OS ITC TT

ABCDEFGHIJKLMNOPQRSTUVWXYZ
abcdefghijklmnopqrstuvwxyz
0123456789

bold

Bodoni SvtyTwo ITC TT

ABCDEFGHIJKLMNOPQRSTUVWXYZ
abcdefghijklmnopqrstuvwxyz
0123456789

bold

Bodoni SvtyTwo SC ITC TT Book

ABCDEFGHIJKLMNOPQRSTUVWXYZ

ABCDEFGHIJKLMNOPQRSTUVWXYZ

0123456789

Book Antiqua

ABCDEFGHIJKLMNOPQRSTUVWXYZ
abcdefghijklmnopqrstuvwxyz
0123456789

bold, *italic,* ***bold italic***

Bookman Old Style

ABCDEFGHIJKLMNOPQRSTUVWXYZ
abcdefghijklmnopqrstuvwxyz
0123456789

bold, *italic,* ***bold italic***

Bordeaux Roman Bold LET

ABCDEFGHIJKLMNOPQRSTUVWXYZ

abcdefghijklmnopqrstuvwxyz

0123456789

Bradley Hand ITC TT

ABCDEFGHIJKLMNOPQRSTUVWXYZ
abcdefghijklmnopqrstuvwxyz
0123456789

Britannic Bold

ABCDEFGHIJKLMNOPQRSTUVWXYZ
abcdefghijklmnopqrstuvwxyz
0123456789

Broadway

ABCDEFGHIJKLMNOPQRSTUVWXYZ
abcdefghijklmnopqrstuvwxyz
0123456789

Brush Script MT

ABCDEFGHIJKLMNOPQRSTUVWXYZ
abcdefghijklmnopqrstuvwxyz
0123456789

Brush Script Std

ABCDEFGHIJKLMNOPQRSTUVWXYZ
abcdefghijklmnopqrstuvwxyz
0123456789

Calibri

ABCDEFGHIJKLMNOPQRSTUVWXYZ
abcdefghijklmnopqrstuvwxyz
0123456789

bold, *italic*, ***bold italic***

Calisto MT

ABCDEFGHIJKLMNOPQRSTUVWXYZ
abcdefghijklmnopqrstuvwxyz
0123456789

bold, *italic*, ***bold italic***

Californian FB

ABCDEFGHIJKLMNOPQRSTUVWXYZ
abcdefghijklmnopqrstuvwxyz
0123456789

bold, *italic*

Cambria

ABCDEFGHIJKLMNOPQRSTUVWXYZ
abcdefghijklmnopqrstuvwxyz
0123456789

bold, *italic*, ***bold italic***

Candara

ABCDEFGHIJKLMNOPQRSTUVWXYZ
abcdefghijklmnopqrstuvwxyz
0123456789

bold, *italic*, ***bold italic***

Cantarell

ABCDEFGHIJKLMNOPQRSTUVWXYZ
abcdefghijklmnopqrstuvwxyz
0123456789

bold, *oblique*, ***bold oblique***

exlijbris.com

CAPITALS

ABCDEFGHIJKLMNOPQRSTUVWXYZ
ABCDEFGHIJKLMNOPQRSTUVWXYZ
0123456789

CASTELLAR

ABCDEFGHIJKLMNOPQRSTUVWXYZ
0123456789

Centaur

ABCDEFGHIJKLMNOPQRSTUVWXYZ
abcdefghijklmnopqrstuvwxyz
0123456789

Century

ABCDEFGHIJKLMNOPQRSTUVWXYZ
abcdefghijklmnopqrstuvwxyz
0123456789

Century Gothic

ABCDEFGHIJKLMNOPQRSTUVWXYZ
abcdefghijklmnopqrstuvwxyz
0123456789

bold, *italic*, ***bold italic***

Century Schoolbook

ABCDEFGHIJKLMNOPQRSTUVWXYZ
abcdefghijklmnopqrstuvwxyz
0123456789

bold, *italic*, ***bold italic***

Chalkboard

ABCDEFGHIJKLMNOPQRSTUVWXYZ
abcdefghijklmnopqrstuvwxyz
0123456789

bold

Charcoal CY

ABCDEFGHIJKLMNOPQRSTUVWXYZ
abcdefghijklmnopqrstuvwxyz
0123456789

Chiller

ABCDEFGHIJKLMNOPQRSTUVWXYZ
abcdefghijklmnopqrstuvwxyz
0123456789

Chopin Script

ABCDEFGHIJKLMNOPQRSTUVWXYZ
abcdefghijklmnopqrstuvwxyz
0123456789

fontsquirrel.com

Cochin

ABCDEFGHIJKLMNOPQRSTUVWXYZ
abcdefghijklmnopqrstuvwxyz
0123456789

bold, *italic*, ***bold italic***

Colonna MT

ABCDEFGHIJKLMNOPQRSTUVWXYZ
abcdefghijklmnopqrstuvwxyz
0123456789

Comfortaa

ABCDEFGHIJKLMNOPQRSTUVWXYZ
abcdefghijklmnopqrstuvwxyz
0123456789

bold

fontsquirrel.com

Consolas

ABCDEFGHIJKLMNOPQRSTUVWXYZ
abcdefghijklmnopqrstuvwxyz
0123456789

bold, *italic*, ***bold italic***

Constantia

ABCDEFGHIJKLMNOPQRSTUVWXYZ
abcdefghijklmnopqrstuvwxyz
0123456789

bold, *italic*, ***bold italic***

Cooper Black

ABCDEFGHIJKLMNOPQRSTUVWXYZ
abcdefghijklmnopqrstuvwxyz
0123456789

Cooper Std

ABCDEFGHIJKLMNOPQRSTUVWXYZ
abcdefghijklmnopqrstuvwxyz
0123456789

italic

COPPERPLATE

ABCDEFGHIJKLMNOPQRSTUVWXYZ
ABCDEFGHIJKLMNOPQRSTUVWXYZ
0123456789

BOLD

COPPERPLATE GOTHIC BOLD

ABCDEFGHIJKLMNOPQRSTUVWXYZ
ABCDEFGHIJKLMNOPQRSTUVWXYZ
0123456789

COPPERPLATE GOTHIC LIGHT

ABCDEFGHIJKLMNOPQRSTUVWXYZ
ABCDEFGHIJKLMNOPQRSTUVWXYZ
0123456789

Corbel

ABCDEFGHIJKLMNOPQRSTUVWXYZ
abcdefghijklmnopqrstuvwxyz
0123456789

bold, *italic*, **bold italic**

Courier

ABCDEFGHIJKLMNOPQRSTUVWXYZ
abcdefghijklmnopqrstuvwxyz
0123456789

bold, *oblique*, ***bold oblique***

Cracked

ABCDEFGHIJKLMNOPQRSTUVWXYZ
abcdefghijklmnopqrstuvwxyz
0123456789

Curlz MT

ABCDEFGHIJKLMNOPQRSTUVWXYZ
abcdefghijklmnopqrstuvwxyz
0123456789

Daniel

ABCDEFGHIJKLMNOPQRSTUVWXYZ
abcdefghijklmnopqrstuvwxyz
0123456789

bold

Diavlo

ABCDEFGHIJKLMNOPQRSTUVWXYZ
abcdefghijklmnopqrstuvwxyz
0123456789

bold exljbris.com

Didot

ABCDEFGHIJKLMNOPQRSTUVWXYZ
abcdefghijklmnopqrstuvwxyz
0123456789

bold, *italic*

DISCO

ABCDEFGHIJKLMNOPQRSTUVWXYZ
abcdefghijklmnopqrstuvwxyz
0 1 2 3 4 5 6 7 8 9

fontsquirrel.com

Edwardian Script ITC

ABCDEFGHIJKLMNOPQRSTUVWXYZ
abcdefghijklmnopqrstuvwxyz
0123456789

Elephant

ABCDEFGHIJKLMNOPQRSTUVWXYZ
abcdefghijklmnopqrstuvwxyz
0123456789

italic

ENGRAVERS MT

ABCDEFGHIJKLMNOPQRSTUVWXYZ
ABCDEFGHIJKLMNOPQRSTUVWXYZ
0123456789

Eras Bold ITC

ABCDEFGHIJKLMNOPQRSTUVWXYZ
abcdefghijklmnopqrstuvwxyz
0123456789

Eras Demi ITC

ABCDEFGHIJKLMNOPQRSTUVWXYZ
abcdefghijklmnopqrstuvwxyz
0123456789

bold, italic, bold italic

Eras Light ITC

ABCDEFGHIJKLMNOPQRSTUVWXYZ
abcdefghijklmnopqrstuvwxyz
0123456789

Eras Medium ITC

ABCDEFGHIJKLMNOPQRSTUVWXYZ
abcdefghijklmnopqrstuvwxyz
0123456789

Facet Block

ABCDEFGHIJKLMNOPQRSTUVWXYZ
abcdefghijklmnopqrstuvwxyz
0123456789

fontfabric.com

FELIX TITLING

ABCDEFGHIJKLMNOPQRSTUVWXYZ
0123456789

Fertigo Pro

ABCDEFGHIJKLMNOPQRSTUVWXYZ
abcdefghijklmnopqrstuvwxyz
0123456789

exljbris.com

FFF Tusj Bold

ABCDEFGHIJKLMNOPQRSTUVWXYZ
abcdefghijklmnopqrstuvwxyz
0123456789

fontsquirrel.com

FLUX ARCHITECT

ABCDEFGHIJKLMNOPQRSTUVWXYZ
ABCDEFGHIJKLMNOPQRSTUVWXYZ
0123456789

BOLD, *ITALIC*, **BOLD ITALIC**

fontsquirrel.com

Fontin Sans

ABCDEFGHIJKLMNOPQRSTUVWXYZ
abcdefghijklmnopqrstuvwxyz
0123456789

bold, *italic*, ***bold italic***, SMALL CAPS   exljbris.com

Footlight MT Light

ABCDEFGHIJKLMNOPQRSTUVWXYZ
abcdefghijklmnopqrstuvwxyz
0123456789

Forte

ABCDEFGHIJKLMNOPQRSTUVWXYZ
abcdefghijklmnopqrstuvwxyz
0123456789

Franklin Gothic Book

ABCDEFGHIJKLMNOPQRSTUVWXYZ
abcdefghijklmnopqrstuvwxyz
0123456789

italic

Franklin Gothic Medium

ABCDEFGHIJKLMNOPQRSTUVWXYZ
abcdefghijklmnopqrstuvwxyz
0123456789

italic

FreeMono

ABCDEFGHIJKLMNOPQRSTUVWXYZ
abcdefghijklmnopqrstuvwxyz
0123456789

bold, *oblique*, ***bold oblique***   savannah.gnu.org

FreeSans

ABCDEFGHIJKLMNOPQRSTUVWXYZ
abcdefghijklmnopqrstuvwxyz
0123456789

bold   savannah.gnu.org

FreeSerif

ABCDEFGHIJKLMNOPQRSTUVWXYZ
abcdefghijklmnopqrstuvwxyz
0123456789

bold, *italic*, ***bold italic***   savannah.gnu.org

Freestyle Script

ABCDEFGHIJKLMNOPQRSTUVWXYZ
abcdefghijklmnopqrstuvwxyz
0123456789

French Script

ABCDEFGHIJKLMNOPQRSTUVWXYZ
abcdefghijklmnopqrstuvwxyz
0123456789

Futura

ABCDEFGHIJKLMNOPQRSTUVWXYZ
abcdefghijklmnopqrstuvwxyz
0123456789

italic

Gentium

ABCDEFGHIJKLMNOPQRSTUVWXYZ
abcdefghijklmnopqrstuvwxyz
0123456789

italic   scripts.sil.org

Gigi

ABCDEFGHIJKLMNOPQRSTUVWXYZ
abcdefghijklmnopqrstuvwxyz
0123456789

bold, italic, bold italic

Garamond

ABCDEFGHIJKLMNOPQRSTUVWXYZ
abcdefghijklmnopqrstuvwxyz
0123456789

bold, *italic*

Geneva

ABCDEFGHIJKLMNOPQRSTUVWXYZ
abcdefghijklmnopqrstuvwxyz
0123456789

Gill Sans

ABCDEFGHIJKLMNOPQRSTUVWXYZ
abcdefghijklmnopqrstuvwxyz
0123456789

bold, *italic*, ***bold italic***

Gill Sans MT

ABCDEFGHIJKLMNOPQRSTUVWXYZ
abcdefghijklmnopqrstuvwxyz
0123456789

bold, *italic*, ***bold italic***

Gill Sans Ultra Bold

ABCDEFGHIJKLMNOPQRSTUVWXYZ
abcdefghijklmnopqrstuvwxyz
0123456789

Gloucester MT Extra Condensed

ABCDEFGHIJKLMNOPQRSTUVWXYZ
abcdefghijklmnopqrstuvwxyz
0123456789

Graublau Web

ABCDEFGHIJKLMNOPQRSTUVWXYZ
abcdefghijklmnopqrstuvwxyz
0123456789

bold

fonts.info

Goudy Old Style

ABCDEFGHIJKLMNOPQRSTUVWXYZ
abcdefghijklmnopqrstuvwxyz
0123456789

bold, *italic*

Haettenschweller

ABCDEFGHIJKLMNOPQRSTUVWXYZ
abcdefghijklmnopqrstuvwxyz
0123456789

Handwriting-Dakota

ABCDEFGHIJKLMNOPQRSTUVWXYZ
abcdefghijklmnopqrstuvwxyz
0123456789

Harlow Solid Italic

ABCDEFGHIJKLMNOPQRSTUVWXYZ
abcdefghijklmnopqrstuvwxyz
0123456789

Harrington

ABCDEFGHIJKLMNOPQRSTUVWXYZ
abcdefghijklmnopqrstuvwxyz
0123456789

Helvetica

ABCDEFGHIJKLMNOPQRSTUVWXYZ
abcdefghijklmnopqrstuvwxyz
0123456789

bold, *oblique*, ***bold oblique***

Helvetica Neue

ABCDEFGHIJKLMNOPQRSTUVWXYZ
abcdefghijklmnopqrstuvwxyz
0123456789

bold, *italic*, ***bold italic***

HERCULANUM

ABCDEFGHIJKLMNOPQRSTUVWXYZ
ABCDEFGHIJKLMNOPQRSTUVWXYZ
0123456789

High Tower Text

ABCDEFGHIJKLMNOPQRSTUVWXYZ
abcdefghijklmnopqrstuvwxyz
0123456789

italic

Hoefler Text

ABCDEFGHIJKLMNOPQRSTUVWXYZ
abcdefghijklmnopqrstuvwxyz
0123456789

italic

Imprint MT Shadow

ABCDEFGHIJKLMNOPQRSTUVWXYZ
abcdefghijklmnopqrstuvwxyz
0123456789

Informal Roman

ABCDEFGHIJKLMNOPQRSTUVWXYZ
abcdefghijklmnopqrstuvwxyz
0123456789

Jazz LET

ABCDEFGHIJKLMNOPQRSTUVWXYZ
abcdefghijklmnopqrstuvwxyz
0123456789

Jokerman

ABCDEFGHIJKLMNOPQRSTUVWXYZ
abcdefghijklmnopqrstuvwxyz
0123456789

Journal

ABCDEFGHIJKLMNOPQRSTUVWXYZ
abcdefghijklmnopqrstuvwxyz
0123456789

fontsquirrel.com

Juice ITC

ABCDEFGHIJKLMNOPQRSTUVWXYZ
abcdefghijklmnopqrstuvwxyz
0123456789

Kingthings Spikeless

ABCDEFGHIJKLMNOPQRSTUVWXYZ
abcdefghijklmnopqrstuvwxyz
0123456789

fontsquirrel.com

Kristen ITC

ABCDEFGHIJKLMNOPQRSTUVWXYZ
abcdefghijklmnopqrstuvwxyz
0123456789

Kunstler Script

ABCDEFGHIJKLMNOPQRSTUVWXYZ
abcdefghijklmnopqrstuvwxyz
0123456789

League Gothic

ABCDEFGHIJKLMNOPQRSTUVWXYZ
abcdefghijklmnopqrstuvwxyz
0123456789

theleagueofmoveabletype.com

Lucida Bright

ABCDEFGHIJKLMNOPQRSTUVWXYZ
abcdefghijklmnopqrstuvwxyz
0123456789

bold, *italic*, ***bold italic***

Lucida Calligraphy

ABCDEFGHIJKLMNOPQRSTUVWXYZ
abcdefghijklmnopqrstuvwxyz
0123456789

Lucida Console

ABCDEFGHIJKLMNOPQRSTUVWXYZ
abcdefghijklmnopqrstuvwxyz
0123456789

Lucida Fax

ABCDEFGHIJKLMNOPQRSTUVWXYZ
abcdefghijklmnopqrstuvwxyz
0123456789

bold, *italic*, ***bold italic***

Lucida Grande

ABCDEFGHIJKLMNOPQRSTUVWXYZ
abcdefghijklmnopqrstuvwxyz
0123456789

bold

Lucida Handwriting

ABCDEFGHIJKLMNOPQRSTUVWXYZ
abcdefghijklmnopqrstuvwxyz
0123456789

Lucida Handwriting Italic

ABCDEFGHIJKLMNOPQRSTUVWXYZ
abcdefghijklmnopqrstuvwxyz
0123456789

Lucida Sans

ABCDEFGHIJKLMNOPQRSTUVWXYZ
abcdefghijklmnopqrstuvwxyz
0123456789

bold, *italic*, ***bold italic***

Lucida Sans Typewriter

ABCDEFGHIJKLMNOPQRSTUVWXYZ
abcdefghijklmnopqrstuvwxyz
0123456789

bold, *oblique*, ***bold oblique***

Lucida Sans Unicode

ABCDEFGHIJKLMNOPQRSTUVWXYZ
abcdefghijklmnopqrstuvwxyz
0123456789

Magneto Bold

ABCDEFGHIJKLMNOPQRSTUVWXYZ
abcdefghijklmnopqrstuvwxyz
0123456789

Maiandra GD

ABCDEFGHIJKLMNOPQRSTUVWXYZ
abcdefghijklmnopqrstuvwxyz
0123456789

Marketing Script

ABCDEFGHIJKLMNOPQRSTUVWXYZ
abcdefghijklmnopqrstuvwxyz
0123456789

fontsquirrel.com

Matura MT Script Capitals

ABCDEFGHIJKLMNOPQRSTUVWXYZ
abcdefghijklmnopqrstuvwxyz
0123456789

Microsoft Sans Serif

ABCDEFGHIJKLMNOPQRSTUVWXYZ
abcdefghijklmnopqrstuvwxyz
0123456789

Miama

ABCDEFGHIJKLMNOPQRSTUVWXYZ
abcdefghijklmnopqrstuvwxyz
0123456789

fontsquirrel.com

Miso

ABCDEFGHIJKLMNOPQRSTUVWXYZ
abcdefghijklmnopqrstuvwxyz
0123456789

bold

fontsquirrel.com

Mistral

ABCDEFGHIJKLMNOPQRSTUVWXYZ
abcdefghijklmnopqrstuvwxyz
0123456789

Modern No. 20

ABCDEFGHIJKLMNOPQRSTUVWXYZ
abcdefghijklmnopqrstuvwxyz
0123456789

Mona Lisa Solid ITC TT

ABCDEFGHIJKLMNOPQRSTUVWXYZ
abcdefghijklmnopqrstuvwxyz
0123456789

Monaco

ABCDEFGHIJKLMNOPQRSTUVWXYZ
abcdefghijklmnopqrstuvwxyz
0123456789

Monotype Corsiva

ABCDEFGHIJKLMNOPQRSTUVWXYZ
abcdefghijklmnopqrstuvwxyz
0123456789

Museo

ABCDEFGHIJKLMNOPQRSTUVWXYZ
abcdefghijklmnopqrstuvwxyz
0123456789

bold   exljbris.com

Museo Sans

ABCDEFGHIJKLMNOPQRSTUVWXYZ
abcdefghijklmnopqrstuvwxyz
0123456789

bold, *italic*, **bold italic**   exljbris.com

NEORETRODRAW

ABCDEFGHIJKLMNOPQRSTUVWXYZ
ABCDEFGHIJKLMNOPQRSTUVWXYZ
0123456789

fontsquirrel.com

NEORETROFILL

ABCDEFGHIJKLMNOPQRSTUVWXYZ
ABCDEFGHIJKLMNOPQRSTUVWXYZ
0123456789

fontsquirrel.com

Niagara Engraved

ABCDEFGHIJKLMNOPQRSTUVWXYZ
abcdefghijklmnopqrstuvwxyz
0123456789

Niagara Solid

ABCDEFGHIJKLMNOPQRSTUVWXYZ
abcdefghijklmnopqrstuvwxyz
0123456789

Note this

ABCDEFGHIJKLMNOPQRSTUVWXYZ
abcdefghijklmnopqrstuvwxyz
0123456789

fontsquirrel.com

OCR A Extended

ABCDEFGHIJKLMNOPQRSTUVWXYZ
abcdefghijklmnopqrstuvwxyz
0123456789

Old English Text MT

ABCDEFGHIJKLMNOPQRSTUVWXYZ
abcdefghijklmnopqrstuvwxyz
0123456789

Onyx

ABCDEFGHIJKLMNOPQRSTUVWXYZ
abcdefghijklmnopqrstuvwxyz
0123456789

Optima

ABCDEFGHIJKLMNOPQRSTUVWXYZ
abcdefghijklmnopqrstuvwxyz
0123456789

bold, *italic*, ***bold italic***

Palace Script MT

ABCDEFGHIJKLMNOPQRSTUVWXYZ
abcdefghijklmnopqrstuvwxyz
0123456789

Palatino

ABCDEFGHIJKLMNOPQRSTUVWXYZ
abcdefghijklmnopqrstuvwxyz
0123456789

bold, *italic*, ***bold italic***

Palatino Linotype

ABCDEFGHIJKLMNOPQRSTUVWXYZ
abcdefghijklmnopqrstuvwxyz
0123456789

bold, *italic*, ***bold italic***

Papyrus

ABCDEFGHIJKLMNOPQRSTUVWXYZ
abcdefghijklmnopqrstuvwxyz
0123456789

Parchment

ABCDEFGHIJKLMNOPQRSTUVWXYZ

abcdefghijklmnopqrstuvwxyz

0123456789

Party LET

ABCDEFGHIJKLMNOPQRSTUVWXYZ

abcdefghijklmnopqrstuvwxyz

0123456789

Perpetua

ABCDEFGHIJKLMNOPQRSTUVWXYZ
abcdefghijklmnopqrstuvwxyz
0123456789

bold, *italic*, ***bold italic***

PERPETUA TITLING MT

ABCDEFGHIJKLMNOPQRSTUVWXYZ
ABCDEFGHIJKLMNOPQRSTUVWXYZ
0123456789

BOLD

Playbill

ABCDEFGHIJKLMNOPQRSTUVWXYZ
abcdefghijklmnopqrstuvwxyz
0123456789

Poor Richard

ABCDEFGHIJKLMNOPQRSTUVWXYZ
abcdefghijklmnopqrstuvwxyz
0123456789

PortagoITC TT

ABCDEFGHIJKLMNOPQRSTUVWXYZ
ABCDEFGHIJKLMNOPQRSTUVWXYZ
0123456789

PRINCETOWN LET

ABCDEFGHIJKLMNOPQRSTUVWXYZ
ABCDEFGHIJKLMNOPQRSTUVWXYZ
0123456789

Pristina

ABCDEFGHIJKLMNOPQRSTUVWXYZ
abcdefghijklmnopqrstuvwxyz
0123456789

Quicksand

ABCDEFGHIJKLMNOPQRSTUVWXYZ
abcdefghijklmnopqrstuvwxyz
0123456789

bold, *oblique*, ***bold oblique***   fontsquirrel.com

Radiohead

ABCDEFGHIJKLMNOPQRSTUVWXYZ
abcdefghijklmnopqrstuvwxyz
0123456789

fontsquirrel.com

Rage Italic

ABCDEFGHIJKLMNOPQRSTUVWXYZ
abcdefghijklmnopqrstuvwxyz
0123456789

Ravie

ABCDEFGHIJKLMNOPQRSTUVWXYZ
abcdefghijklmnopqrstuvwxyz
0123456789

Rockwell

ABCDEFGHIJKLMNOPQRSTUVWXYZ
abcdefghijklmnopqrstuvwxyz
0123456789

bold, *italic*, ***bold italic***

Rockwell Condensed

ABCDEFGHIJKLMNOPQRSTUVWXYZ
abcdefghijklmnopqrstuvwxyz
0123456789

bold

Rockwell Extra Bold

ABCDEFGHIJKLMNOPQRSTUVWXYZ
abcdefghijklmnopqrstuvwxyz
0123456789

Saginaw

ABCDEFGHIJKLMNOPQRSTUVWXYZ
abcdefghijklmnopqrstuvwxyz
0123456789

bold

fontsquirrel.com

Savoye LET

ABCDEFGHIJKLMNOPQRSTUVWXYZ
abcdefghijklmnopqrstuvwxyz
0123456789

Sansation

ABCDEFGHIJKLMNOPQRSTUVWXYZ
abcdefghijklmnopqrstuvwxyz
0123456789

bold   fontsquirrel.com

Santa Fe LET

ABCDEFGHIJKLMNOPQRSTUVWXYZ
abcdefghijklmnopqrstuvwxyz
0123456789

Schoolhouse Cursive B

ABCDEFGHIJKLMNOPQRSTUVWXYZ
abcdefghijklmnopqrstuvwxyz
0123456789

Schoolhouse Printed A

ABCDEFGHIJKLMNOPQRSTUVWXYZ
abcdefghijklmnopqrstuvwxyz
0123456789

Script MT Bold

ABCDEFGHIJKLMNOPQRSTUVWXYZ
abcdefghijklmnopqrstuvwxyz
0123456789

Segoe UI

ABCDEFGHIJKLMNOPQRSTUVWXYZ
abcdefghijklmnopqrstuvwxyz
0123456789

bold, *italic*, ***bold italic***

SHOWCARD GOTHIC

ABCDEFGHIJKLMNOPQRSTUVWXYZ
0123456789

Snap ITC

ABCDEFGHIJKLMNOPQRSTUVWXYZ
abcdefghijklmnopqrstuvwxyz
0123456789

Snell Roundhand

ABCDEFGHIJKLMNOPQRSTUVWXYZ
abcdefghijklmnopqrstuvwxyz
0123456789

bold

STENCIL

ABCDEFGHIJKLMNOPQRSTUVWXYZ
ABCDEFGHIJKLMNOPQRSTUVWXYZ
0123456789

Stone Sans ITC TT

ABCDEFGHIJKLMNOPQRSTUVWXYZ
abcdefghijklmnopqrstuvwxyz
0123456789

SYbIL GREEN

aBCDEFGHIJKLMNOPQRSTUVWXYZ
abcdEFGHIJKLMNOPQRSTUVWXYZ
0123456789

fontsquirrel.com

Symbol

ΑΒΧΔΕΦΓΗΙϑΚΛΜΝΟΠΘΡΣΤΥςΩΞΨΖ
αβχδεφγηιφκλμνοπθρστυϖξψς
0123456789

SYNCHRO LET

ABCDEFGHIJKLMNOPQRSTUVWXYZ
ABCDEFGHIJKLMNOPQRSTUVWXYZ
0123456789

Tahoma

ABCDEFGHIJKLMNOPQRSTUVWXYZ
abcdefghijklmnopqrstuvwxyz
0123456789

bold

Tempus Sans ITC

ABCDEFGHIJKLMNOPQRSTUVWXYZ
abcdefghijklmnopqrstuvwxyz
0123456789

Times

ABCDEFGHIJKLMNOPQRSTUVWXYZ
abcdefghijklmnopqrstuvwxyz
0123456789

bold, *italic*, ***bold italic***

TitilliumText14L

ABCDEFGHIJKLMNOPQRSTUVWXYZ
abcdefghijklmnopqrstuvwxyz
0123456789

200, 400, **600**, **800**   fontsquirrel.com

Tw Cen MT

ABCDEFGHIJKLMNOPQRSTUVWXYZ
abcdefghijklmnopqrstuvwxyz
0123456789

bold, *italic*, ***bold italic***

Tw Cen MT Condensed

ABCDEFGHIJKLMNOPQRSTUVWXYZ
abcdefghijklmnopqrstuvwxyz
0123456789

bold

UglyQua

ABCDEFGHIJKLMNOPQRSTUVWXYZ
abcdefghijklmnopqrstuvwxyz
0123456789

italic

fontsquirrel.com

UNIVERSAL FRUITCAKE

ABCDEFGHIJKLMNOPQRSTUVWXYZ
ABCDEFGHIJKLMNOPQRSTUVWXYZ
0123456789

fontsquirrel.com

Vegur-Bold

ABCDEFGHIJKLMNOPQRSTUVWXYZ
abcdefghijklmnopqrstuvwxyz
0123456789

fontsquirrel.com

Viner Hand ITC

ABCDEFGHIJKLMNOPQRSTUVWXYZ
abcdefghijklmnopqrstuvwxyz
0123456789

Vivaldi Italic

ABCDEFGHIJKLMNOPQRSTUVWXYZ
abcdefghijklmnopqrstuvwxyz
0123456789

Vladimir Script

ABCDEFGHIJKLMNOPQRSTUVWXYZ

abcdefghijklmnopqrstuvwxyz

0123456789

Walkway Bold

ABCDEFGHIJKLMNOPQRSTUVWXYZ

abcdefghijklmnopqrstuvwxyz

0123456789

fontsquirrel.com

Wide Latin

ABCDEFGHIJKLMNOPQRSTUVWXYZ

abcdefghijklmnopqrstuvwxyz

0123456789

Yanone Kaffeesatz

ABCDEFGHIJKLMNOPQRSTUVWXYZ

abcdefghijklmnopqrstuvwxyz

0123456789

bold

fontsquirrel.com

Zag

ABCDEFGHIJKLMNOPQRSTUVWXYZ

abcdefghijklmnopqrstuvwxyz

0123456789

bold

fontfabric.com

INDEX

{ speaking in styles }

FUNDAMENTALS OF CSS *for* WEB DESIGNERS

jason cranford teague

New Riders

VOICES THAT MATTER™

{ Speaking in Styles aims to help Web designers learn the "language" that will be used to take their vision from the static comp to the live Internet. Many designers think that CSS is code, and that it's too hard to learn. Jason takes an approach to CSS that breaks it down around common design tasks and helps the reader learn that they already think in styles—they just need to learn to speak the language.

Jason helps Web designers find their voice, walks them through the grammar of CSS, shows them how to write their design specs in CSS, and how to prepare it for screen, printer, or handheld devices. Along the way designers will learn to optimize their code, make it accessible, optimize for search engines, mix it up with Flash, and more. }

Jason Cranford Teague
ISBN: 0-321-57416-8 • 360 pages • June 2009

newriders.com

New Riders

0 1341 1319860 7

Safari
Books Online

RECEIVED

MAR 0 3 2011

HUMBER LIBRARIES
LAKESHORE CAMPUS

DISCARD

Get free online access to this book for 45 days!

And get access to thousands more by signing up for a free trial to Safari Books Online!

With the purchase of this book you have instant online, searchable access to it for 45 days on Safari Books Online! And while you're there, be sure to check out Safari Books Online's on-demand digital library and their free trial offer (a separate sign-up process). Safari Books Online subscribers have access to thousands of technical, creative and business books, instructional videos, and articles from the world's leading publishers.

Simply visit www.peachpit.com/safarienabled and enter code IJZIAZG to try it today.